# The Challenge of Old Testament Women 1

# The Challenge of Old Testament Women 1

A Guide for Bible Study Groups

## Sara Buswell

**BAKER BOOK HOUSE**
Grand Rapids, Michigan 49506

ISBN: 0-8010-0928-6

*Fifth printing, November 1989*

Scripture quotations, unless otherwise indicated,
are taken from the New International Version.
Copyright 1973, 1978, 1984 by New York International Bible Society.
Used with permission of Zondervan Bible Publisher.

Printed in the United States of America

Cover art: Pompeo Batoni, Italian.
*Esther Before Ahasuerus*, oil on canvas
Philadelphia Museum of Art:
Gift of the Women's Committee
of the Philadelphia Museum of Art
in honor of their 100th anniversary.
Used with permission.

To
my family

for the glory of God

# Contents

# Foreword

This book is an invitation to meet women of the Old Testament, and to apply principles of God's character and design seen in them to your own personality and circumstances. The text and study questions are intended to facilitate your acquaintance with these women who, after all, are not very different from yourself. To be a woman today, pleasing to God and transformed to the image of his likeness, is a high calling, a real challenge. But God has not left us without models to warn and to welcome us along the way.

This book assumes an inductive format for study. To consider each of the thirteen women, first read the

Scripture passage and supplementary verses along with the study-discussion questions. Be aware of the questions as you study the Scripture passages. When you have formulated your own initial answers, discuss them with a friend or a group, if possible. Then read the chapter, which may offer you new direction and challenge, and possibly give new ideas for answers to the questions. Where verses are quoted directly from the Bible, the New International Version has been used, unless otherwise indicated.

The relevance of each Bible character to the needs of each reader will be different. You may not agree with the applications suggested by other members of your group or in the printed text of this book. That is not important. What matters is that you grow closer to God as you realize that his Word is living and active, and that he desires to make himself known to you personally. As you become acquainted with these women, your relationship with the Lord will deepen as well.

Speaking personally, I want to mention that the women in this book were first introduced to me in my Jewish home and synagogue as figures of more or less historical or spiritual value. But not until I had committed my life to Jesus Christ was I able to read the Bible for myself with any degree of appreciation. After several years, I went back to the Old Testament in search of my roots and found there a number of women with whom I could identify and through whom I could better understand my own identity in the Lord. I also discovered that the teachings of Christ and of Paul in the New Testament were helpful in con-

firming God's principles through the characters of
these women. I pray that you will find this study just
as meaningful as you seek to discover yourself
through the Bible.

Sara Buswell

# Study Plan

1. Read the questions at the beginning of each lesson.
2. Read the Scripture passage(s) listed and be aware of the questions as you read. Allow time to think about words or phrases or incidents that are especially meaningful to you. Underline them in your Bible.
3. Formulate initial answer(s) to questions.
4. If possible, discuss answers with a friend or group.
5. Read the lesson commentary.
6. Revise answers, if necessary.
7. Apply your answers to your life as God directs.

## PART ONE

# Women of Obedience

Ruth
Sarah
Esther

Whom must I obey, and when? Are the expectations and requirements the same for every person and every situation? The answers to such questions as these are crucial to our relationship with God and with our society. In the Bible we find God's specific commands as well as the consequences for choosing or failing to obey him (see Deut. 30:15–20). God also gives us many examples of individuals whose experiences and development may help us to understand and apply his principles to our own lives, even though our circumstances may be very different.

God is eminently worthy of our obedience.

Whether willfully or in spite of ourselves, however, we frequently fail to obey him (Rom. 7:15–25). A further problem arises when we try to differentiate between obedience to God and obedience to other people. Sometimes God tests and trains us by allowing us to be in situations in which we must submit to the authority of another individual, in order that we learn to depend on and yield to God's supreme authority in a new and deeper way. At other times we must deal directly with him alone. And sometimes it seems that what God requires is in direct opposition to what others demand of us. We certainly need his wisdom to discern and follow his principles.

Perfect obedience must be voluntary, not forced. It requires inner affirmation as well as overt behavior. Each party, the commander and the submitter, must respect and value the other and self. Obedience at its best is a two-way relationship of trust, not just an "I say, you do" dictatorship.

Ruth, Sarah, and Esther had to learn how to live with a mother-in-law, a husband, and a king, respectively. They demonstrated true commitment, but not always total compliance, while they grew in understanding of God's expectations. As we consider their circumstances and their characters, we will gain insight that will challenge our own preconceptions and practices of obedience.

# 1
## Ruth

**Primary Scripture Reading**

Book of Ruth

**Supplementary References**

Genesis 19
Numbers 25
Judges 3
Matthew 1:5

John 14:15
Romans 8:28
Philippians 2:5–11
Colossians 3:23-24

**Questions for Study and Discussion**

**1.** Read and enjoy the whole Book of Ruth. Which people did Ruth obey, and how often? Of what significance is the fact that she was not an Israelite but a Moabite? What other factors might have made it difficult for Ruth to obey Naomi?

**2.** Describe your relationship to your in-laws, other relatives, friends, or co-workers to whom you are responsible. How does it compare with that of Ruth and Naomi? What principles underlying their relationship could you apply to your situation, and with what positive results?

**3.** Compare Orpah's response to Naomi with that of Ruth. Which course do you think you might have taken, and why?

When have you obeyed either minimally or maximally, and with what results? Under what conditions do you find obedience fulfilling or frustrating?

**4.** How do you connect the requirement of obedience to God with obedience to people, both in principle and in your practical experience? Do you think your attitude or act of obedience has served as a testimony to a relative or friend? How have you used Christ's example of submission to strengthen or comfort you?

**5.** What about the men in this story? Do you think Elimelech acted obediently in his decision to go to Moab in the first place? What happened for good or for bad as a result?

**6.** Give several instances that demonstrate Boaz's obedience to God throughout this story. How, do you think, did this character trait encourage Ruth to obey both him and God? Briefly describe some key men or women in your life who impressed you by their obedience to God and tell how this has helped develop the trait of obedience in you.

**7.** Do you find any negative qualities in Ruth's character? How can you apply the outstanding experiences in her life to your own situation? List several blessings Ruth received for her obedience. How have you been similarly blessed?

Ruth and Esther are the only two books in the Bible named for women, and both have much to teach us about obedience. In our own time, when the role of mother-in-law is widely mocked and daughters-in-law are often disrespectful, the model relationship between Ruth and Naomi is especially valuable. But Ruth's story is more than a handbook on how to get along with one's in-laws. It celebrates the gentle beauty of love and loyalty between individuals, and it demonstrates the positive power of obedience to God for both personal fulfillment and wider blessing. By committing herself to Naomi as well as to Naomi's God, Ruth found satisfaction in service. Instead of losing her identity by her voluntary and complete submission, Ruth's place was joyfully confirmed.

## Surprising Obedience

The harmony between Ruth and her mother-in-law is even more appealing when we consider two unusual factors that could have driven them apart:

> Now Elimelech, Naomi's husband, died, and she was left with her two sons. They married Moabite women, one named Orpah and the other Ruth. After they had lived there about ten years, both Mahlon and Kilion also died, and Naomi was left without her two sons and her husband (Ruth 1:3–5).

Mahlon, the natural connecting link between Ruth and Naomi, was dead. Nothing specific is mentioned about the way the two women got along with each other while he was alive during those ten years in Moab. Instead, the account begins with the development of their relationship after Mahlon's death and at the time of the women's departure for Judah. This fact invites me to consider my relationship with my mother-in-law. Do we function together only because of and through the mediation of my husband, her son? Or can we develop a friendship for its own sake, one of wide and lasting substance for our mutual benefit that goes beyond our having Jamie in common?

The second potentially divisive factor was that Ruth was a Moabite. A brief review of the history of this neighboring nation proves that its land and people were clearly off limits for the Hebrews. The founding father Moab was the result of Lot's incestuous union with his older daughter (Gen. 19:37). Though Moab was not on the list of nations to be entirely destroyed by the Israelites under Joshua, its idolatrous practices were particularly offensive and troublesome (Num. 25). Judges 3 relates that Eglon, king of Moab, received power from the Lord to punish Israel for eighteen years. When his people again cried out to him, God raised up the judge Ehud, who killed Eglon and defeated Moab, thus establishing peace for eighty years.

The Book of Ruth begins, "In the days when the judges ruled," placing it within this period. Elimelech's decision to take his family into Moab to escape the famine in Israel probably occurred at a time when Moab was subdued, or at least not openly hostile toward Israel. Nevertheless, God had repeatedly warned the Israelites not to mingle, intermarry, or otherwise join in the wicked practices of alien nations. The fact that both Naomi's sons chose Moabite women for wives shows that they did not heed these instructions, if indeed they had received them. It also indicates the attractiveness of these foreign influences to the Israelites, a temptation from which God desired to shield them. But we also see his mercy in grafting into his line of blessing one Moabite because of her faith and obedience.

Naomi had two daughters-in-law, Ruth and Orpah. In view of their position as Moabite widows, it may seem that Orpah's decision to return to her own mother's house was more natural than Ruth's when Naomi announced her determination to go back to Bethlehem. We might even argue that Orpah, after politely offering to accompany Naomi, was acting in accord with her mother-in-law's wishes by remaining in Moab with her own people. Ruth, on the other hand, "clung to her" and stubbornly refused to leave Naomi. But Orpah's obedience can only be called superficial, or minimal. Her offer was made out of duty, not devotion, and Naomi discerned and declined it as such. Orpah's name means "stubbornness," and nothing more is said of her after she kissed Naomi farewell. In contrast, Ruth, whose name means "friendship," remained to finish her story and claim a place in the genealogy of David and ultimately of Christ (Matt. 1:5).

## Witness in Obedience

Ruth did more than merely remain with Naomi; she was in fact her main support, both during their journey and after their arrival in Israel, even though she was the stranger in Bethlehem. News of her faithfulness circulated quickly and preceded her into the fields of Boaz. When she asked why he was being so kind to a foreigner, Boaz replied,

I've been told all about what you have done for your mother-in-law since the death of your husband—how

you left your father and mother and your homeland
and came to live with a people you did not know before (Ruth 2:11).

Though directly attracted by her outward beauty and
manner, Boaz was already aware of her reputation for
loyal love and service. Boaz told her, "All my fellow
townsmen know that you are a woman of noble
character" (Ruth 3:11).

Here we see the powerful testimony of Ruth's relationship with Naomi. Her unselfish devotion to one
person, characterized by her obedience, made her appealing to another person and to a whole community.
However, Ruth did not flaunt her obedience as long-
suffering, but held it in her heart as love. She was not
looking for praise or pity, and she seemed surprised
that her service had been observed. Not once did she
begrudge Naomi's leadership or bemoan her own circumstances. Instead of bitterness there was beauty, in
her attitude as well as on her face. Ruth found her
obedience fulfilling. Her immediate and ultimate rewards far exceeded anything she could have antici-
pated or desired.

## Wholeness of Obedience

How did Ruth's obedience come to have such a tremendous impact on those around her? It started with a
personal commitment, a permanent decision that
brought her peace and provided her with direction for
all that followed. On the boundary of Moab, Ruth had
told Naomi,

Don't urge me to leave you or turn back from you.
Where you go I will go, and where you stay I will stay.
Your people will be my people and your God my God.
Where you die I will die, and there I will be buried.
May the LORD deal with me, be it ever so severely, if
anything but death separates you and me (Ruth
1:16–17).

This was not a marriage vow; yet, how many of us have
used these words in our own weddings, and how
strong our families would be if we lived them! In my
case, I married my husband because his God had become my God, and so we could commit our life together into his care.

Ruth's commitment was absolute. Rather than con-
straining her, it created new purpose and opportunity
for developing her character. When they arrived in
Bethlehem, Ruth volunteered to glean, saying, "Let
me go to the fields and pick up the leftover grain behind anyone in whose eyes I find favor" (Ruth 2:2).
Naomi accepted with the simple words, "Go ahead,
my daughter." When she returned, Ruth shared her
grain with Naomi and gave an account of the day's
events. Then it was Naomi who sensed God's direction
and gave Ruth detailed instructions as to how to approach Boaz, which Ruth obeyed with perfect results
(Ruth 3:1–6). Ruth 4:17 indicates that after Ruth's future and family were secure, Naomi was included in
the household redeemed by Boaz, for when the neigh-
bors noticed how much she cared for Obed they said,
"Naomi has a son." Truly, the deepest love, trust, and
respect were at the center of the relationship of these
women, which brought their mutual fulfillment.

As Ruth obeyed Naomi, so she obeyed Boaz, both at their first meeting and later at the threshing floor. She won the admiration of both Naomi and Boaz as much by the quickness of her unquestioning responses as by her completeness in carrying out commands.

Although I believe that my own children are entitled to know my good reasons behind instructions I give them, sometimes it comes as a delightful surprise to find them trusting my wisdom and benevolence enough to accept my orders without demanding "Why?" But then, haven't we all said to other people, as I certainly have on occasion, "Of course I'm willing to help, but you'll have to tell me *why* you want it done this way"? We measure out our cooperation in proportion to our understanding of and agreement with their desires. Isn't it refreshing and challenging to find no such spirit in Ruth? She won respect because she offered her respect in the form of obedience.

## Worship by Obedience

The product of Ruth's obedience was Obed, the child fathered by Boaz as kinsman-redeemer, the one who would inherit the family land and name in place of Naomi's deceased husband and sons. Obed means "worship" in Hebrew. Is not obedience really the outward action that derives from the inner response of faith, love, and trust practiced in regard to individuals and ultimately God? Christ said, "If you love me, you will obey what I command" (John 14:15). Ruth's acts of obedience throughout her story may be interpreted as practical acts of worship of the God she had made her own by faith.

In this light we must evaluate our obedience toward those in positions of authority over us. Is it freely offered? Is it maximal like Ruth's, or minimal like Orpah's? If we are afraid to yield in obedience to another person, we can draw comfort and confidence from the Lord himself, knowing that he can be fully trusted in all things to work "for the good of those who love him, who have been called according to his purpose" (Rom. 8:28). Realizing that it is God who controls every aspect of our lives, are we not safe in his hands, and in the hands of those whom by his sovereign will we are directed to obey?

But let us be honest. Some people are easier to obey than others, either because of their personalities or ours. We are not always free to choose whom and when we are to obey. Perhaps the situation is difficult, one in which submission is demanded when trust has not yet been established. Instead of dwelling on the shortcomings of people who wield authority, we do well to yield to God's perfect love, faithfulness, and trustworthiness. Remember that Jesus did not hold himself above obedience, but gave his life in demonstration of total submission to his Father.

Your attitude should be the same as that of Christ Jesus:

Who, being in very nature God, did not consider equality with God something to be grasped,

25

but made himself nothing, taking the very nature
  of a servant, being made in human likeness.
And being found in appearance as a man, he
  humbled himself and became obedient to death—
  even death on a cross!
Therefore God exalted him to the highest place
  and gave him the name that is above every name,
that at the name of Jesus every knee should bow,
  in heaven and on earth and under the earth,
and every tongue confess that Jesus Christ is Lord,
  to the glory of God the Father (Phil. 2:5–11).

As Christ did, as Ruth did, let us ask God to work in us to transform our feeble gestures of human obedience into acts of divine worship. We can find delight in serving the Lord, instead of indulging in resentment over subservient relationships. The result will be inner freedom and release from bitterness, and also a powerful testimony to those exercising authority and to outside observers as well. Just as Ruth's attitude of obedience toward Naomi moved Boaz and all Bethlehem, the Holy Spirit will enable us to move others. Paul taught the church at Colossae:

Whatever you do, work at it with all your heart, as working for the Lord, not for men, since you know that you will receive an inheritance from the Lord as a reward. It is the Lord Christ you are serving (Col. 3:23–24).

While we obey others we can joyfully remember that it is God alone who is worthy of complete obedience. When our confidence in him is reflected in our submission to others we become living testimonies to our trust in God's perfect plan. If we follow Ruth's beautiful example, someone may examine our stories and find the witness, the wholeness, and the worship in our lives of obedience.

# 2

## Sarah

### Primary Scripture Reading

Genesis 11–23

### Supplementary References

Deuteronomy 28:9–10
Ezekiel 36:23–36
John 3:5–8

Ephesians 2:1–10;
  5:22–33
Hebrews 11:6–19
1 Peter 3:1–7

### Questions for Study and Discussion

**1.** Skim the Genesis chapters, noting highlights of Sarah's life, particularly her name change in Chapter 17. What was Sarah's greatest desire? What did she decide to do about it? Whose help did she solicit? What were the immediate and long-range consequences of her effort? Does God need your help in order to fulfill his Word, and if so, what kind of help?

**2.** Why, do you think, did God change Abram's name to Abraham, and Sarai's to Sarah (Gen. 17:5, 15)? Do you find any resulting changes in their personalities or conduct? How has God quickened you, in the sense of giving you new life, since you have become identified with his name?

**3.** In Genesis 12 and 20, Abraham told Sarah to lie to two heathen rulers. What was the lie, and how serious were the consequences in each instance? What was Abraham forgetting? How do you think you would handle a similar situation in which your husband, parent, or boss wanted you to tell a lie to protect him or her?

**4.** Genesis 18:15 relates that Sarah told another lie, which was not prompted by her husband. What was the situation? Why, do you think, did she lie? What did she learn from this experience?

**5.** What differences do you detect between Abraham's laughter in Genesis 17:17 and Sarah's laughter in 18:12? Why did they name their baby Isaac? When have you laughed in response to God's promises? Did you laugh because of joy or unbelief? What happened?

**6.** Compare Genesis 16:4–6 with 21:8–13. If God told your husband to do whatever you said (as he told Abraham to do in the second passage), what responsibility would that put on you? How did this command work out for Abraham and Sarah? Considering the relationship between this husband and wife, why, do you think, did Peter suggest Sarah as a model for wives because she "obeyed Abraham, calling him lord" (1 Peter 3:1–6)?

**7.** List as many of God's promises to Abraham and Sarah as you can find. What does the New Testament say about their response to the promises? What promises of God are you claiming for your present situation? Are you expecting a miracle? How can you demonstrate your faith and obedience to God in seemingly impossible circumstances?

"Laughter, the Best Medicine" is more than a popular feature in *Reader's Digest*—it describes common experience. But did you know that laughter can also be a symptom of serious spiritual disorder?

God used laughter at a crucial moment in Sarah's life to uncover a root of bitterness and unbelief and to promote the healing process of submission. If we could chart her growth from expedience to obedience, we would note several ups and downs rather than a steady curve. This holds true even after God changed the names of Abram and Sarai to Abraham and Sarah, symbolizing with the Hebrew letter *h* the Spirit's breathing life into their beings. Although they gradually came to understand more of God's promises and power, Sarah and Abraham occasionally reverted to a former level of selfishness and lack of faith through fear. The laughter occurred at the midpoint of their development, and was in response to God's personal revelation.

We might like to think that from the moment God changed Sarah and Abraham's names, or from the time when the Holy Spirit first enters a believer today, there should be no further problems with the old nature—that the switch from villainy to victory should be instantaneous and permanent. But this ideal is no more true for us than it was for Sarah and Abraham; and rightly so, for the concept of obedience includes a real choice at every step. Each one of us has the same potential as they for either fruitfulness or failure, for we sometimes depend on God and sometimes on our own ambitions and abilities to gain our desires.

## No Laughing Matter

Abram and Sarai had a serious problem, which is mentioned at the onset and repeated during their history to show its importance:

> Terah became the father of Abram, Nahor, and Haran. . . . Abram and Nahor both married. The name of Abram's wife was Sarai. . . . Now Sarai was barren; she had no children (Gen. 11:27–30).

> Now Sarai, Abram's wife, had borne him no children (Gen. 16:1).

Ten years had elapsed between these two statements, and fourteen years more were to pass before Sarah finally, at age ninety, gave birth to Isaac. In her culture a lack of children was considered equivalent to a lack of favor with God. Prosperity was measured as much by the size of one's family as by material possessions (see Ps. 127:3–5). Even though Abram had by this time accumulated great wealth "in livestock and in silver and gold" (Gen. 13:2), he still had no offspring. What was the point of material expansion if there would be no future generation in whom to invest this treasure?

More confusing was the fact that God kept promising Abram an heir; in fact, he promised him many nations and rich blessings. Was God delaying out of weakness and needed Abram and Sarai's help to accomplish his purposes by any and all means? Or was he perhaps waiting for Abram and Sarai to show some initiative before he would act in their behalf? Does God help those who help themselves, or only those who depend solely on his help? Did the way in which God gradually unfolded his plans serve as an invitation to their further faith and friendship, or did it continue to simply tease and frustrate Abram and Sarai? How can we apply God's power and promises today, and what does he ask of us in return for his favor?

Let us look at the sequence of God's promises to Abram and Sarai and consider whether they laid claim to them or contradicted them by their actions. We will also examine the relationship between Abram and Sarai as a model of support and submission within marriage.

First, God said,

> "Leave your country, your people and your father's household and go to the land I will show you.
>> I will make you into a great nation and I will bless you;
>> I will make your name great, and you will be a blessing.
>> I will bless those who bless you, and whoever curses you I will curse;
>> and all peoples on earth will be blessed through you" (Gen. 12:1–3).

Later he elaborated concerning the offspring and the land of promise. Even with these assurances, Abram was still unsure about the way in which God would fulfill his word, so he asked about it.

> But Abram said, "O Sovereign LORD, what can you give me since I remain childless and the one who will inherit my estate is Eliezer of Damascus?" And Abram said, "You have given me no children, so a servant in my household will be my heir" (Gen. 15:2–3).

Notice the hint of impatience and the wrong conclusion Abram drew as to what God intended. Therefore, God added,

"This man will not be your heir, but a son coming from your own body will be your heir." He took him outside and said, "Look at the heavens and count the stars—if indeed you can count them." Then he said to him, "So shall your offspring be" (Gen. 15:4–5).

In response to this promise, Abram finally released his fear and placed his faith in God. "Abram believed the LORD, and he credited it to him as righteousness" (Gen. 15:6). God then confirmed his covenant and Abram's faith by sending a "smoking fire pot with a blazing torch" to pass between two piles of sacrificed animals, sealing the contract unilaterally. Then he gave a detailed prophecy:

"Know for certain that your descendants will be strangers in a country not their own, and they will be enslaved and mistreated four hundred years. But I will punish the nation they serve as slaves, and afterward they will come out with great possessions. You, however, will go to your fathers in peace and be buried at a good old age. . . . To your descendants I give this land, from the river of Egypt to the great river, the Euphrates. . . . (Gen. 15:13–21).

The promise was now very specific, but there was still no mention of Abram's marriage partner. Sadly, almost reproachfully, Sarai concluded that she was not to be an active participant in producing the promised seed through her own body. Notice the beginning of Chapter 16:

Now Sarai, Abram's wife, had borne him no children. But she had an Egyptian maidservant named Hagar; so she said to Abram, "The LORD has kept me from having children. Go, sleep with my maidservant; perhaps I can build a family through her" (Gen. 16:1–2).

Thus, impatience gave way to expedience as Sarai resorted to her own methods and resources to produce a child according to the flesh. We may sympathize with her innocence or ignorance in not knowing the miracle God yet had in store for her, but we cannot really justify the fact that she never asked him for clarification or comfort. Hagar conceived and bore the child Ishmael, and learned an important lesson in submission when she was confronted by "the God who sees me" (Gen. 16:13).

But Sarai was still barren. The only fruits of her self-effort were jealousy, bitterness, blame, and cruelty, which came after Abram abdicated his authority with the words, "Your servant is in your hands. . . . Do with her whatever you think best" (Gen. 16:6). It would take thirteen years of silence in the Scripture record before they were ready for God's next revelation of himself and the miracle of his life-giving power. Each of us would do well to examine our own actions for traces of self-centered expedience rather than full obedience to God.

Today it is just as difficult to know when to take initiative and when to wait expectantly for the fulfillment of God's promises as it was for Abraham and Sarah. Without knowing the future or being able to control all of the factors affecting the behaviors of everyone involved in a decision, how can we choose correctly among alternatives? How can I know what God wants me to do or not to do? That is the question facing all of us and, praise God, we can have help and hope to find the answers, if we ask ourselves:

1. Are my motives self-seeking or God-serving? Am I acting out of fear or faith, pride or praise to God? Am I really trying to gain something for myself or to give all the glory to God?
2. Are my methods consistent with God's character and standards as revealed in his Word? Am I applying appropriate Scripture principles to my situation?
3. Have I asked God to guide me through specific answers to prayer and the comforting peace of the Holy Spirit (Phil. 4:6–7)? How can I monitor the situation and modify my actions as God directs?

If I consider the why, what, and how of my actions in this way, I can be confident that God will rebuke or rescue me if I misstep, and that he will protect and prosper my walk of obedience.

## Laughing Place

For years I puzzled over the fact that when Abraham laughed in response to God's renewal of the covenant and promise of a child to Sarah, he was met with an assurance of God's blessing for Ishmael and a repetition of the covenant with Isaac (Gen. 17:17). But Sarah laughed in almost the same way when she heard the promise concerning her son, and she was rebuked. Why did the Lord rebuke one and reward the other for the same natural reaction? The answer may be found in the heart's response to God in these two individuals, and in the position each one took when he spoke to them. Let us place the texts side by side. In Chapter 17, we read in part:

When Abram was ninety-nine years old, the LORD appeared to him and said, "I am God Almighty; walk before me and be blameless. I will confirm my covenant between me and you and will greatly increase your numbers." Abram fell facedown, and God said to him, "As for me, this is my covenant with you: You will be the father of many nations. No longer will you be called Abram; your name will be Abraham, for I have made you a father of many nations. . . .As for you, you must keep my covenant, you and your descendants after you for the generations to come. This is my covenant you are to keep: Every male among you shall be circumcized. . . .God also said to Abraham, "As for Sarai your wife, you are no longer to call her Sarai; her name will be Sarah. I will bless her and will surely give you a son by her. I will bless her so that she will be the mother of nations; kings of peoples will come from her." Abraham fell facedown; he laughed and said to himself, "Will a son be born to a man a hundred years old? Will Sarah bear a child at the age of ninety?" And Abraham said to God, "If only Ishmael might live under your blessing!" Then God said, "Yes, but your wife Sarah will bear you a son, and you will call him Isaac. I will establish my covenant with him as an everlasting covenant for his descendants after him.

And as for Ishmael, I have heard you: I will surely bless him. . . . But my covenant I will establish with Isaac, whom Sarah will bear to you by this time next year" (Gen. 17:1–21).

In Chapter 18, Abraham offered hospitality to three visitors who turned out to be two angels and the Lord himself:

While they ate, he stood near them under a tree. "Where is your wife Sarah?" they asked him. "There, in the tent," he said. Then the LORD said, "I will surely return to you about this time next year, and Sarah your wife will have a son." Now Sarah was listening at the entrance to the tent, which was behind him. Abraham and Sarah were already old and well advanced in years, and Sarah was past the age of childbearing. So Sarah laughed to herself as she thought, "After I am worn out and my master is old, will I now have this pleasure?" Then the LORD said to Abraham, "Why did Sarah laugh and say, 'Will I really have a child, now that I am old?' Is anything too hard for the LORD? I will return to you at the appointed time next year and Sarah will have a son." Sarah was afraid, so she lied and said, "I did not laugh." But he said, "Yes, you did laugh" (Gen. 18:8–15).

The notes of cynicism and fear in Sarah's laughter and lie are absent from Abraham's response. He expressed, "Wow!" while she seemed to say, "Hah!" The underlying question was the same for both of them: How could such a thing happen after so long a time? But their expectations and their postures were opposite. Abraham fell facedown in reverent submission, while Sarah stood at the tent door in disbelief. It was no surprise to Abraham that God could read his mind and respond to his inner laughter—that was the way in which God had always communicated with his friend. But stunned silence prevailed when Sarah finally and fully absorbed the fact that here before her was God himself, who could penetrate to the very core of her private pain, giving her the ability to fully trust him at the same time as he enabled her to bear life. Hebrews 11:6 states, "And without faith it is impossible to please God, because anyone who comes to him must believe that he exists and that he rewards those who earnestly seek him."

Sarah did not really seek the Lord until she stopped looking for solutions to her problems within herself; when she sought him, he found her and brought her to himself in full faith and in fulfillment of all his promises. Do not we, too, think some things are too hard for the Lord, or too small for him to bother with?

## Laughing Boy

A promise has value only if it is believed and kept. Enjoy the joy bubbling through Sarah and Abraham over the birth of Isaac, whose name means "laughter."

Now the LORD was gracious to Sarah as he had said, and the LORD did for Sarah what he had promised. Sarah became pregnant and bore a son to Abraham in his old age, at the very time God had promised him. Abraham gave the name Isaac to the son Sarah bore him. When his son Isaac was eight days old, Abraham circumcized him, as God commanded him. Abraham was a hundred years old when his son Isaac was born to him. Sarah said, "God has brought me laughter, and everyone who hears about this will laugh with me." And she added, "Who would have said to Abraham that Sarah would nurse children? Yet I have borne him a son in his old age" (Gen. 21:1–7).

When we fully recognize God as our Lord, and receive his Spirit by faith, we can join fully in Sarah's laughter.

We have seen that obedience to God requires faith *in* God. The real miracle of Isaac's birth was the quickening of faith that enabled Abraham and Sarah to generate new life from their old bodies. Similarly, our faith in God's faithfulness to fulfill his promises gives us the power and the purpose for obedience. Without such faith we have neither the reason nor the resource to obey. Ezekiel 36:36 affirms the basis of our faith: "I the LORD have spoken, and I will do it!" And 1 Thessalonians 5:24 agrees: "The one who calls you is faithful and he will do it."

Our salvation is secured not by our feeble grasp on God but by his strong grip on us. The ability to believe comes not from ourselves but from the Holy Spirit (John 3:6). Otherwise we would have no hope, no power for life. Yet, we have a choice of whether or not to receive and obey his Word to us, just as Sarah and Abraham did, when we are confronted with the reality of our human limitations and God's limitless love. For them the circumcision of Isaac, and later Abraham's willingness to sacrifice his son if God commanded it, sealed the covenant. Today, as then, God asks for the circumcision of our hearts, not just our bodies (Deut. 30:6). In faith and in action, we should strive to cut ourselves off from sin and cling to the cross.

The recognition of God's authority and Sarah's response of obedience were essential prerequisites to the arrival of Isaac, the promised seed. There is another aspect of Sarah's submission that is important for us to consider: the relationship between husband and wife. Peter points to Sarah as a model:

> Wives, in the same way be submissive to your husbands so that, if any of them do not believe the word, they may be won over without talk by the behavior of their wives. . . . Your beauty should not come from outward adornment, such as braided hair and the wearing of gold jewelry and fine clothes. Instead, it should be that of your inner self, the unfading beauty of a gentle and quiet spirit, which is of great worth in God's sight. For this is the way the holy women of the past who put their hope in God used to make themselves beautiful. They were submissive to their own husbands, like Sarah, who obeyed Abraham and called him her master. You are her daughters if you do what is right and do not give way to fear (1 Peter 3:1–6).

The issue of submission is as relevant for A.D. 2000 as it was nearly 2000 years before Christ. Actually, I am not convinced that when Sarah called Abraham "my master" in Genesis 18:12 she was speaking with only pure love and respect in her voice. There was at least a tinge of sarcasm there. Nor can I believe that it was right for Sarah to submit in silence to Abraham when he resorted to expedience out of fear and first told a

41

pharaoh in Egypt and then Abimelech, king of Gerar, that Sarah was his sister. But it is interesting to note a difference in their relationship before and after God confronted Sarah with his personal, powerful, probing presence in the face of her need (Gen. 18). When they were acting outside of God's will (Gen. 16), Sarai blamed Abram for the failure of her scheme, and he gave Hagar into her hands. Persecution of the servant resulted. After the birth of Isaac, there was a different outcome of their discussion concerning Hagar:

> The child grew and was weaned, and on the day Isaac was weaned Abraham held a great feast. But Sarah saw that the son whom Hagar the Egyptian had borne to Abraham was mocking, and she said to Abraham, "Get rid of that slave woman and her son, for that slave woman's son will never share in the inheritance with my son Isaac." The matter distressed Abraham greatly because it concerned his son. But God said to him, "Do not be so distressed about the boy and your maidservant. Listen to whatever Sarah tells you, because I will make the son of the maidservant into a nation also, because he is your offspring" (Gen. 21:8–13).

This time Abraham was encouraged to listen to his wife's advice because she was sensitive and submissive to God's will. Protection resulted for both sons and for Sarah as well, as her obedience to God increased her influence for good with her husband.

Each individual is accountable to God for the measure and nature of his or her obedience in every situation. Sarah's example challenges me to know and obey God, who knows me perfectly, so that in his power I can walk before him and be blameless and fruitful. I want to cooperate with my husband so that together we can discern God's will and go his way as a family. Then I am truly Sarah's daughter, as well as her namesake, if I "do what is right and do not give way to fear."

How might fearing for your personal safety or guarding what brings you satisfaction overshadow your faith and joy in your loving Savior? When God speaks to you, do you respond with the laughter of reverent submission, or the laughter of rebellion? In what ways is your relationship to the important people in your life a reflection of your obedience to God?

# 3
## Esther

**Primary Scripture Reading**

Book of Esther

**Supplementary References**

Deuteronomy 30:1–6          1 Timothy 2:1–4
Psalms 25, 27, 37, 62       Hebrews 13:17
Matthew 22:15–21            1 Peter 2:13–17

### Questions for Study and Discussion

**1.** Read the entire Book of Esther. Why, do you think, is God's name not mentioned in it? Trace proofs of his presence and power behind the scenes. How are you aware of his control over seeming coincidences in your life?

**2.** What is your attitude toward the law of the land? Do you obey it perfectly (including all traffic and tax laws)? Is there a time when you feel you need not or ought not obey the law? What guidelines do the above New Testament passages offer?

**3.** Why, do you think, did Queen Vashti defy the king's command? What personal rights do you claim? Whose rights have you stood up for, and with what results? How do you feel about a husband's right to be "ruler over his own household" (Esther 1:22)?

**4.** What risks did Esther face in choosing to obey God's call? What risks were there in refusing? How do you evaluate the risks of alternatives you face?

**5.** When and why have you kept secret your identity as a Christian (see Esther 2:20)? Did your action bring either honor or dishonor to God? What did you learn from the experience?

**6.** Why did God allow Esther, a beautiful and believing Jewish virgin, to be taken into the harem of a pagan despot? How do Genesis 50:9–10 and 2 Corinthians 4 help you understand God's character and methods at work to accomplish his purposes in unusual ways (see also Isa. 55:8–11)? How is God using circumstances of your life for training or blessing yourself and other people, which might be similar to the way he brought Esther to the palace "for such a time as this" (Esther 4:14)?

**7.** What do you know of God's perfect timing to accomplish his will as you have waited for him? What do you think of Esther's strategy to expose Haman? How do you balance patience with action as you seek to serve God in obedience (consider Pss. 25, 27, 37, and 62)?

Ruth's obedience was a sincere and beautifully attractive expression of her love for Naomi and for her God. Sarah's obedience was sealed by God's powerful, personal confrontation, which transformed her natural dependence on her own resources into a deep faith in his power alone. In Esther's story we have an opportunity to consider obedience toward the law, as well as in marriage and family relationships. We shall consider the requirement, the risk, and the reward of obedience, both for Esther and for ourselves.

The book of Esther is a holiday story. Each year at the Jewish Festival of Purim in late winter, the special scroll, or *Megillah*, is read in the synagogue. Every time the name of Haman, the villain, is mentioned, the whole congregation responds by hissing, and whirring raucous noisemakers called greggors. There is a joyous carnival atmosphere, with costume parades, games, and a sense of exhilaration as the story of the triumph of good over evil is retold. Family members exchange gifts, and baskets of food are brought to the poor, both in accordance with the details of the celebration decreed in Esther 9:22. Purim has no counterpart on the Christian calendar. But underneath the jubilation of special songs, traditional foods (triangular fruit-filled tarts called *hamantaschen*, or Haman's hats), and religious services, a tense drama is replayed, in which the heroine Esther saved her exiled people from total annihilation in the sixth century B.C.

## Requirements of Obedience

Notice first the expectation of subservience in the social and legal context of Esther's day. Everyone in the empire had to obey the king of the Medes and Persians, Xerxes (or Ahasuerus), without question or delay. He himself was subject only to the law of the Medes and Persians, which could never be altered. When Queen Vashti refused to display herself in front of King Xerxes' banquet guests, she broke the law by defying his command. Such a violation threatened the whole system. In persuading him to take the severest possible action against her, his counselors expressed another fear:

> "For the queen's conduct will become known to all the women, and so they will despise their husbands and say, 'King Xerxes commanded Queen Vashti to be brought before him, but she would not come.' This very day the Persian and Median women of the nobility who have heard about the queen's conduct will respond to all the king's nobles in the same way. There will be no end of disrespect and discord" (Esther 1:17–18).

As long ago as 2500 years, there was considerable anxiety concerning a husband's authority and his wife's obedience within the home. These nobles made sure that dispatches were circulated to every province and in every language, proclaiming each man to be ruler over his own household. We do not know whether or not the directive achieved its purpose, but we can see that the question of obedience in marriage, which is also critical in our society, is hardly a new one.

We can also see the emphasis on obedience to the law. Besides the human actors in the Book of Esther, the law of the Medes and Persians played a crucial role in the drama. Evolved over a period of centuries as the Persian Empire gained supremacy over more and more territory (to the point of encompassing 127 provinces from India to Ethiopia by Esther's time), this legal system was ironclad. Every person in the empire was only too well aware of the dire consequences of violating its decrees, yet it was so complex that nearly everyone could be found guilty of some infraction. Once a decree was issued, it might never be amended or revoked, not even by the king himself. (This law of the Medes and Persians made a lot of trouble for Daniel, too. See Daniel 6, for example.) It was this law that sealed Queen Vashti's doom and that Haman tried to invoke to eliminate all the Jews. Fortunately, Haman's plan was thwarted by a higher law.

In reference to this higher law, it is curious that God's name is not mentioned once in the Book of Esther. Writers generally offer two reasons for this omission. Remember that the events of Esther occurred during the period of the Babylonian exile, which followed the defeat of Jerusalem in 586 B.C. This was a very low moment in Jewish history, when God's positive involvement in the lives of his people might have seemed both less apparent and less appreciated than during times of conquest. It is possible that some Jews found it easier to imagine that God was either impotent to help or else that he had abandoned them, and they chose to drop his name from their conversations and writings, rather than to face the fact that God had warned them specifically and repeatedly of the inevitable outcome of their continued disobedience to his law (see Deut. 30:1–6). But in fact, the tone of the Book of Esther is one of joy and victory, even at times of great fear and stress. God was not helpless, nor did he refuse to help.

A better explanation is that the omission of God's name was precautionary. The book closes with the Jews still in exile, safe but not free, with no assurance of when they might return to their homeland. They were wise to rejoice without seeming to gloat over their success, lest new plots arise against them. Persecution at the hands of stronger and more numerous enemies was always a possibility, and in fact proved to be a reality too often in Jewish history. What is beautiful to realize—and the pleasure is as real for believers today as it was for faithful Jews of Esther's day—is how mightily and mercifully God controlled events to care for his people both as individuals and as a nation, and how ultimately he received the glory by preserving his record in his Word.

A passage crucial to our considering God's requirement of obedience is Esther 4:13–16, which includes the appeal Esther's elder cousin Mordecai brought to her, and her response:

> "Do not think that because you are in the king's house you alone of all the Jews will escape. For if you remain silent at this time, relief and deliverance for the Jews will arise from another place, but you and your father's family will perish. And who knows but that you have come to royal position for such a time as this?" Then Esther sent this reply to Mordecai: "Go, gather together all the Jews who are in Susa, and fast for me. Do not eat or drink for three days, night or day. I and my maids will fast as you do. When this is done, I will go to the king, even though it is against the law. And if I perish, I perish."

The first principle to realize is that God gives every individual choices. He does not manipulate anyone into accomplishing his purposes against his or her will. The Lord has much to teach and to give us, but he waits until we are willing to learn and receive it. Second, we should count it a great privilege to serve him in the ways he directs us, but we must also recognize that he is never helpless, whether or not he has our help. If we refuse the opportunity to obey, he will simply achieve his plans through someone else. His will *shall* be done, but we will miss the blessing. Mordecai made this point clear to Esther when he stated that her family would perish if she remained silent, while God would still send relief from another place. The potential loss was consequence enough for Esther, who took the risk of presenting herself before the king without being summoned, an act that demanded the death penalty according to the law of the Medes and Persians.

## Risk of Obedience

Esther dared to approach the king uninvited. How did she become queen in the first place? Vashti had taken a risk also, by standing up for her rights and refusing to appear when the king had summoned her. Apparently, it was nearly as dangerous not to come when invited as to come uninvited! Vashti summarily lost her position for the sake of her principles. We should take a moment to consider whether she was right in the stand she took. She dared to insist on being treated with respect as an individual person of value, and not merely as one more bauble among the king's vast treasures to be displayed. It is difficult for us today to identify with the circumstances of her culture, yet I suppose that Vashti would undoubtedly receive sympathetic support for her ideals, if not for her actions, even though she lost her case in the court. Vashti's example deserves some attention, if not a separate chapter of study. Is hers the kind of self-expression for which we should be striving? Is it our rights or God's righteousness for which we must take a stand? In this book we are studying the women of the Old Testament in order to understand ourselves in the context of God's principles and possibilities. If we come to know who we are—individuals created in his image and for his glory—we shall develop a better sense of which rights are worth defending. What are you willing to risk, and for what purpose?

King Xerxes was not entirely pleased with the course of action he had followed in dealing with Queen Vashti. Several years later, after losing a war with Greece (historically placed between Chapters 1 and 2 of Esther), he remembered with regret the events that led to the loss of his queen. But the law of the Medes and Persians gave him no option by which to restore her to his side. To cheer him a grand beauty contest was announced throughout the kingdom, with the winner to be declared the new queen. The beautiful young Jew Esther was chosen as a candidate and placed in the preliminary harem at Susa, the capital of the kingdom. She immediately gained the favor of the eunuch Hegai, manager of the harem, who saw to it that she received all the benefits of special food and beauty treatments during the twelve months of preparation for her one-night tryst with the king.

During that time, however, Esther was careful to obey Mordecai's orders not to disclose her identity as a Hebrew. In fact, Esther 2:20 indicates the extent to which obedience was a lifelong trait of this maiden:

> But Esther had kept secret her family background and nationality just as Mordecai had told her to do, for she continued to follow Mordecai's instructions as she had done when he was bringing her up.

Verse 7 explains that Mordecai had become Esther's guardian when her parents died some years earlier. Thus he represented the extent of Esther's family ties. She was already accustomed to obeying his wise and loving commands without question, trusting him to guide her.

Mordecai had a keen perception of whom and when to obey. He had uncovered and reported a plot to assassinate the king, an act of loyalty that was duly recorded and later rewarded. As a Jew, however, he had stoutly refused to bow down in homage to any man. This refusal so enraged the prime minister Haman that he swore to destroy not only Mordecai but every Jew in the kingdom. Mordecai's counsel to Esther when she entered the harem was not that she should resist the flow of events that would bring her to the king's bed, but that she should preserve the secret of her identity until the most advantageous time for her people and for herself. Mordecai was not a rebel. He was willing to abide by and support the system of government under which he lived, especially in order to achieve the protection of his people. But he had to take a stand against human authority when it infringed upon his primary obligation to obey God, his supreme authority. For that he would take any risk, and he encouraged Esther to do the same.

The turning point in Esther's story came as she chose to accept and fulfill the obligation of obedience to God. Once Mordecai opened Esther's eyes to the danger and the duty facing her, and to the critical role she could play in behalf of her people, she acted decisively to conceive and carry out her plan. Her first step was to call for a three-day fast of all the Jews in Susa. Well aware that she would be breaking the civil law, she asked her people to petition God to overrule that law with his divine protection. She placed herself in the hands of the highest authority, risking all to obey him. We would do well not only to admire, but also to apply Esther's process of patience, prayer, and planning as she carried out her purpose under God.

Seeing Esther move through the precarious schedule of invitations, petitions, and revelations recorded in Chapters 5–8 of the story, we must be impressed with her poise and strength derived from her decision to rely on God and speak boldly for her people. She made no brash demands, issued no statements of defiance, and threw no fits of hysteria. Her beauty, calm, and sincere respect continued to attract the king, who was most eager to discover and fulfill the desire of her heart. She offered hospitality to Xerxes and Haman the second time and waited confidently for God to show her the perfect moment and manner in which to expose her news and her need—that Haman had twisted the inviolable law of the Medes and Persians to serve his own vanity by ordering the annihilation of the entire Jewish population. Esther was not set on challenging the authority of her king and husband. Her mission was much more urgent—to work within her proper position of queen to rescue her people. Her courage and faith in God empowered her to succeed where other methods and motives would surely have collapsed in failure.

Can you triumph in your situation by means of a solid confidence that God has indeed appointed you to serve him in your place at "such a time as this"? Will you put your faith in his ability to guide and strengthen you with his wisdom and love? In what ways do you need to grow in discernment regarding when to submit to those in authority over you and when to act boldly, always in obedience to God's principles rather than in service of your own pride? Esther's example provides a beautiful model to encourage and challenge each of us.

## Reward for Obedience

Because Esther's cause was just, her timing perfect, and her God omnipotent, she accomplished her goal. Haman's wicked plot to hang Mordecai and murder all of the Jews came down on his own head, for he was hanged on the same gallows he had prepared for his enemy. The law now authorized the Jews to defend themselves against their would-be attackers on the specified days of slaughter. While they took revenge, however, they refused to take plunder from the Persians, in acknowledgment of God's help. Thus, the days Haman had chosen for their deaths they dedicated to joyful feasting and celebration—from that time to the present. The king elevated Mordecai to a position of greatness, and Esther was recognized as a sensitive and wise ruler along with her husband, to the great relief of all her people. The Book of Esther ends exuberantly:

> Mordecai the Jew was second in rank to King Xerxes, preeminent among the Jews, and held in high esteem by his many fellow Jews, because he worked for the good of his people and spoke up for the welfare of all the Jews (Esther 10:3).

The immediate results of Esther's obedience were indeed remarkable and are certainly worthy of annual celebration, even in our own day. But I believe she enjoys further honor by pointing the way for us to determine practical principles of obedience in our own lives, whenever we feel bound by uncomfortable constraints of a rigid chain of command. Esther could have felt caught between the social expectations to obey her cousin Mordecai on the one hand and her husband Xerxes on the other; or between the king of the Medes and Persians and the king of heaven and earth. Is it possible to follow a right course among such seemingly conflicting demands today? Esther's story shows us the possibility of an affirmative answer. She met such a challenge with quiet and consistent courage. She challenges us to persevere in our circumstances, focusing on God's purposes "for such a time as this," for the blessing of others as well as for our personal benefit. Instead of experiencing frustration and conflict over the constraints in our lives, we may discover that God's righteous requirement of obedience offers the rewards of rest and redemption if we are willing to place our faith wholly in him.

## PART TWO

# Women of Disobedience

Eve

Lot's Wife

Of course we want to learn from women in the Old Testament who obeyed God, but why should we spend time on the negative examples of disobedience? We can learn not to follow them. Obeying God requires a submissive spirit that recognizes and responds to his will. In contrast, instances of disobedience, whether in outright rebellion or more subtle disregard of his law, reveal a hardened heart that fails to take God's Word seriously and insists on its right to independent action and interpretation.

Our real concern in this section, as we consider Eve and Lot's wife, is not so much that they sinned, but that each of us is likely to commit the same errors. The consequences of their disobedience were severe—the introduction of pain and death, rejection from Paradise, and physical petrification.

Do these extreme punishments really fit the seemingly simple crimes of a bite of fruit and a backward glance? We must believe that they do, and that God's warnings are to be taken as seriously as his promises. Only then can we appreciate his character as a holy God of truth and begin to approach him with reverent submission. It is not enough to claim we believe *in* God when in fact we have not bothered to hear or heed his instructions. We must believe God. These two women, and many others, did not.

# 4
## Eve

### Primary Scripture Reading

Genesis 1–4

### Supplementary References

Psalm 119:41–42; 145:3
Isaiah 55:8–9
Matthew 4:1–11;
    25:10–30

Ephesians 5:22–23;
    6:10–18
1 Timothy 2
James 4:7

### Questions for Study and Discussion

**1.** Why did God create Adam? Why did he create Eve? What do you think it means to be a helpmeet (Gen. 2:18, KJV)? In your life does the helpmeet concept perhaps apply to situations other than marriage? How can you do better at this assignment?

**2.** Do you think of yourself as being God's helper? What kind of help does he need from you (consider Matt. 25 for your answer)?

**3.** What special purposes and privileges do you enjoy as a woman? What do Ephesians 5:22–33 and 1 Timothy 2 say about a woman's place? How do you feel about your place in your family, church, job, and community?

**4.** Why did God command Adam not to eat from the tree of the knowledge of good and evil? Do you think Eve understood this command? Why was the tree in the garden in the first place? If God knew Adam and Eve would disobey, why did he allow them to be tempted by the serpent?

**5.** God cursed Adam "because you listened to your wife." What influence do you have on your family members and close acquaintances through your attitudes, words, and actions? How can you develop a more godly influence?

**6.** Have you ever compelled someone over whom you have influence to pay more attention to your words than to God's Word? Does that person trust you? Should he or she? How can you encourage him or her to follow God's commands when the wisdom of your human counsel is questionable?

**7.** Eve succumbed to the serpent's temptation because she changed, added to, and failed to understand God's word. Describe a similar experience in which you have yielded to temptation. How was Christ able to stand firm against Satan's attacks (Matt. 4)? How can you be more victorious over temptation in the future? What specific commands and promises of Scripture might you memorize to help you deal with temptation?

Five times in Genesis 1 God saw that his creation was good. At the end of the chapter "God saw all that he had made, and it was very good." Then Genesis 2 gives greater details about Adam and Eve and their placement in the Garden of Eden. Here, God's command, his comment, and the couple's response all include negative words: "you must not eat," "it is not good," "they felt no shame." Even before the introduction of sin in Genesis 3, we may sense that something is about to go wrong.

What did God have in mind when he created Eve? Did she turn out the way he intended? How could she have avoided falling for the subtle serpent's sinister suggestions? How can we find and follow God's good and perfect will (see Rom. 12:1–2) when we are tempted to disobey? We have much to learn about God, about Satan, and about ourselves as we consider this First Lady of Disobedience, Eve.

## Creation of a Helper

When I was about six years old, I enjoyed watching my mother in the kitchen. Everything she did looked easy and fun, and I wanted to help. She let me take over each task while she started on something else. Within a few minutes I would discover that the job I had taken wasn't easy or fun for me, because I lacked my mother's strength and experience. But what she was doing at *that* moment looked really easy and fun! Again, she let me take over. I followed her around the kitchen for an hour, peeling, beating, cracking, or chopping for a minute or two and then giving up.

My mother had to come back and finish everything herself. She might have enjoyed training me, but she also had a responsibility to get dinner on the table. She would say, "I know you want to help, but this is not helping."

Now I say to my own two helpers, "It is only helping if you are really helping." I try to give them jobs that are easy and fun and within their range of success.

God wants us to be his helpers in much the same way. We need to learn, as Sarah did, that we are helping him best when we fulfill only the tasks he has assigned to us, no more and no less.

Of course, helping God almost always involves helping others as well. When God first observed, "It is not good for the man to be alone" (Gen. 2:18), he brought all the beasts and birds to Adam "to see what he would name them. But for Adam no suitable helper was found" (Gen. 2:19–20); so he created woman to be man's *helpmeet* (the word used in KJV). The idea was not merely to provide the man with either a subordinate or a second self, but to create a true companion, one who would be both compatible and compassionate, a full partner in all his joys and sorrows, one with whom he would be able to share himself fully and whom he could fulfill.

More than just an old-fashioned synonym for wife, the word *helpmeet* describes the supporting role of all Christians. Hebrews 10:24–25 reminds us, "Let us consider how we may spur one another on toward love and good deeds. Let us not give up meeting together, as some are in the habit of doing, but let us encourage one another—and all the more as you see the Day aproaching." To be a helpmeet in this broader sense is to be of service to all people, whatever our relationship. When we love others in God's name we do not lose our individuality but discover our true identity as his helpers.

### Command to Obey

In the sequence of Genesis 2, God told Adam about the forbidden fruit (v. 17) before he created Eve (v. 22).

And what did she learn about this crucial command? God's words to Adam were:

> You are free to eat from any tree in the garden; but you must not eat from the tree of the knowledge of good and evil, for when you eat of it you will surely die (Gen. 2:16–17).

But in Genesis 3:2–3, Eve told the serpent:

> We may eat fruit from the trees in the garden, but God did say, "You must not eat fruit from the tree that is in the middle of the garden, and you must not touch it, or you will die."

What differences are there between these two statements, and do they matter? Which verses give the more accurate rendition of God's command?

At first glance, these two passages seem to be saying about the same thing. But they do not. The differences become clear when we chart the verses side by side.

| Genesis 2:16–17 | Genesis 3:2–3 |
| --- | --- |
| You are free to eat from any tree in the garden | We may eat fruit from the trees in the garden |
| but you must not eat from the tree | but God did say, "You must not eat fruit from the tree |
| of the knowledge of good and evil | that is in the middle of the garden |
| | and you must not touch it |

| | |
|---|---|
| for when you eat of it | or |
| you will | you will |
| surely | |
| die. | die." |

God told Adam that the tree embodied the knowledge of good and evil, but Eve told the serpent only that it was in the middle of the garden. If she was aware of the power of the tree, she did not use this information to help herself resist the power of Satan, who was only too glad to substitute his own cunning version of God's intent:

> For God knows that when you eat of it your eyes will be opened, and you will be like God, knowing good and evil (Gen. 3:5).

Thus, Eve yielded the security and strength that come only from God's exact words, and Satan moved in. Of course, this does not mean that Biblical principles cannot be applied to various circumstances and needs today. But we must be very sure to base our applications on a deep and faithful understanding of God's Word. Accept no substitutes.

Eve's second big mistake was to add to God's command. God had not said that the tree could not be touched. How can we be sure of this? Is it not possible that the phrase was simply left out of Genesis 2:17, and that Eve's quotation was really the more complete? The answer is no, for two reasons. First, when God found Adam and Eve in the garden after their fall into sin, he said to them, "Have you eaten from the tree that I commanded you not to eat from?" (Gen. 3:11). And in cursing Adam he added the explanation, "Because you listened to your wife and ate from the tree about which I commanded you, 'You must not eat of it'" (Gen. 3:17). If God had actually commanded them not to touch the tree, he would have mentioned the fact. Besides, God had placed Adam in the garden "to work it and take care of it" (Gen. 2:15), which must have included permission to touch the trees when necessary.

Second, the whole Bible helps us to know that God is not so arbitrary as Eve makes him appear in her statement. Although his ways are not our ways (Isa. 55:8–9), and his greatness is beyond what we can fathom (Ps. 145:3), we can have confidence that he has perfect, not petty reasons for all he does and says. Eve's adding to his command renders it almost frivolous, and again reveals her lack of deep understanding of God's design.

Perhaps we at times also fail to understand God's design. How can we resist temptation better than Eve did? By asking God for fuller understanding of his purposes, and by simply obeying better, whether or not we are granted such illumination. In the desert Christ became our perfect model when he countered each of Satan's insidious propositions with direct quotations from the Scriptures (Matt. 4:1–11). The result: Satan fled. Though Jesus was aware that he had all the power of the universe at his disposal to claim or renounce his kingdom at any moment, he submitted perfectly to his Father's plan and timing at every step. To resist Satan he used only the resource we, too, have been given—the Word of God. He knew it perfectly, for he *is* the Word. He did not alter or add to it in any way. We, too, must commit ourselves to storing his Word in our hearts daily, so that we may be well–armed against temptation (consider Eph. 6:10–18, Ps. 119, James 4:7). The moment of attack is not the time to begin making weapons; we must study and pray continually. Only then can we hope to face temptation by the power of God's Word with more confidence and strength than Eve displayed.

## Corruption

There is another aspect of Eve's disobedience from which we can learn something important. Having succumbed to temptation, how did Eve persuade Adam to eat the fruit with her? Having become corrupt, how did she corrupt her husband also? The key verse is tantalizingly stark: "She also gave some to her husband, who was with her, and he ate it" (Gen. 3:6).

Parenthetically, it may be that this verse raises more questions in our minds than it resolves. Was Adam with her during her encounter with Satan? Why didn't he speak up to protect her or himself? There is certainly no indication that Adam protested or tried to discover the source of the fruit Eve offered him. Was this because he already knew where it came from, since he was there all along, and was only holding back until he was satisfied that nothing terrible seemed to happen when his wife took that first bite?

But let us make two observations about Eve from this verse. Eve did not appear to resort to devious means to persuade Adam to taste the fruit after her. She simply gave it to him and he ate it. Adam trusted his wife perfectly. Of course, with no sin in the world prior to that moment, he would have had no reason not to trust her. Nevertheless, this scene moves me to treasure the high degree of trust my husband has placed in me. We ought not treat lightly the trust people have in us. We should strive to be worthy of it every day, not by merely refraining from bald deception, but by unfailingly encouraging them to do good, and by serving their needs in little as well as big matters.

The second observation about Eve concerns the amount of influence she had over her husband because of their mutual love and trust. He did what she said.

When I step off the curb, my children follow me into the street, trusting that I have indeed checked for traffic. When I give my opinion on whether it would be better at this time to remodel the kitchen than to buy a new car, my husband trusts my advice. These responses from my family are in one sense gratifying, but in another sense they represent a tremendous responsibility. What if I am mistaken in my judgment, in these examples as well as in countless others? Obviously, my children could get hit by a truck, or our budget could be thrown seriously out of balance (not to mention what could happen to our poor old car). I am not the head of the household, yet my family is greatly affected by what I do and say.

And what of my power to destroy a friendship, degrade a minister, dampen a social occasion, or deflate a child's enthusiasm simply by dropping a comment or a sigh into the conversation around the dinner table? I can corrupt those around me just by projecting my own foul mood, for whatever reason. This realization challenges me to gain better control over my thoughts and feelings, as well as my words and deeds, lest I tempt anyone to evil because of our shared relationship of trust.

## Consequences

Eve was created to be a suitable helper for Adam. She failed because she did not take God's command seriously enough either to obey it or to depend on it as a strong defense against temptation. She corrupted her husband. What were the consequences? It is not difficult to list quite a few.

1. The possibility of sin entered the world. (Gen. 3:6)
2. Adam, Eve, and Satan were cursed by God. (Gen. 3:14–19)
3. Christ's ultimate victory was foreshadowed. (Gen. 3:15)
4. Pain in childbirth was increased. (Gen. 3:16)
5. Women were placed under their husbands' rule. (Gen. 3:16)
6. Adam and Eve were cast out of Eden, which was sealed against them. (Gen. 3:24)
7. Adam stopped listening to Eve.

But wait! How can I say Adam stopped listening to Eve when I have just finished saying that we women have a great deal of influence over those who trust our words and deeds, and that we ought to be more mindful of that fact? Because I want to make another point here: Adam's big mistake was in obeying his wife *instead of God*. Before the Lord laid his curse on Adam, he said, "Because you listened to your wife and ate from the tree about which I commanded you, 'You must not eat of it'" (Gen. 3:17). Having violated Adam's trust in her, Eve had lost something precious for all time. Adam would have to be more careful from that time forward to check everything for himself. The once-perfect helpmeet was henceforth placed under the rule of her husband, and God made it crystal clear that his Word was the only one that must be adhered to. Is it not also necessary for us to guard against placing those who trust us in the position of having to choose between God's Word and our selfish interests?

It is not easy to speculate on what life in Eden might have been like—a perfect paradise without sin, no sickness or hurt, no fear or doubt. We can only guess as to what could have happened if Eve had resisted Satan, or if Adam had resisted Eve. God is both wise and merciful in not revealing to us too much of that early perfection, since it is so difficult for us sinful beings to comprehend. Yet, there is enough in these first few chapters of the Bible to keep us thinking and growing each time we read them. Obviously, we have not dealt here with every issue concerning Eve that has been raised throughout the centuries. But for me her disobedience represents a challenge to know and stand firmly on the Word of God, and to seek his help against all temptation, for my own good as well as for the sake of my family.

Perhaps you have disobeyed God's Word because you, like Eve, have not known God well enough to take him at his word. Have you diluted the power of the Scriptures to half-strength through your own selections, additions, and transformations, so that you have no defense against temptation when it comes? Then you must choose to take a new direction by drawing comfort and strength from Christ's perfect example of obedience and resistance.

> May your unfailing love come to me, O LORD,
>    your salvation according to your promise;
> then I will answer the one who taunts me,
>    for I trust in your word (Ps. 119:41–42).

# 5

## Lot's Wife

### Primary Scripture Reading

Genesis 11–19

### Supplementary References

Deuteronomy 17
1 Kings 10–11
Isaiah 1:9
Matthew 5:13; 10:15
Luke 12, 17

John 3, 14
Romans 9
1 Corinthians 3:15
2 Corinthians 12
Revelation 11:8

### Questions for Study and Discussion

**1.** Why did God destroy Sodom and Gomorrah? Was he acting in anger or in mercy, do you think? (Consider Gen. 14, 18, and 19.)

**2.** Is God "Judge of all the earth" (Gen. 18:25)? How does he judge your life? What excuses do you offer for your sins? How will you escape destruction?

**3.** What commands did the angels give to Lot? What reasons did God have for these commands? How obedient was Lot? How was his entire family affected by his actions?

**4.** Where, do you think, did Lot find his wife in the first place? What criteria would he have used in choosing a woman to marry?

**5.** Where is your treasure, and thus your heart? How trapped are you by your appetites, accumulated possessions, personal affections? If your city were about to blow up, what or whom would you try to save?

**6.** Why did Jesus say, "Remember Lot's wife" (Luke 17:32)? What applications was he making, based on her story? How does his reference affect the historicity of Genesis 19?

**7.** Examining your response to God, might you be a pillar of salt, or the "salt of the earth" (Matt. 5:13)? Do you look backward to the things you had or were, or are you focusing on God's blessings to come? How can you turn yourself in the right direction?

Jesus said, "Remember Lot's wife." Yet, we are never told her name, she has no speaking part in the Bible, and she is mentioned in only a few verses. How can we remember a woman about whom we know so little, and why is she so important?

We can find additional clues to this woman's personality by examining the character of her family and city, and we can learn several significant principles from her disobedience and her destruction. Her husband Lot, who was Abraham's nephew, was an individual who thought primarily of his own needs and desires. When Abraham offered him first choice of all the land he could see, Lot immediately chose the greenest pastures for himself. In Genesis 19, he appeared to value his angelic visitors more highly than

74

his own family, opting to offer his daughters to the rioting Sodomites rather than to violate his code of hospitality. Lot's failures cannot be denied, even in regard to his own selfish goals. Having picked the best land, Lot had to be rescued and restored to it by Abraham in a counterattack against the pagan kings. Later Lot's guests had to reach out to retrieve him and strike the rioters with blindness in order to protect him and his household. Lot's best efforts to convince his future sons-in-law to leave Sodom were rejected as being weak humor. The last scene in which we see Lot is filled with drunkenness and incest. Surely he is one of the most pitiable characters in the Bible.

What about Sodom? Genesis 19:5 makes it obvious that homosexuality was practiced openly there, and we have evidence of other sexual sins as well. Passages in Isaiah (1:9), Matthew (10:15), Romans (9:29), and Revelation (11:8) indicate the proverbial depravity of the place, which is supported by other historical writings and archaeological findings. When the Lord made a special visit to determine whether the outcry against Sodom was warranted, he could not find even ten righteous people for whom to save it. Still, Lot chose to live there and immerse himself and his family in that ungodly environment. He even rose to a position of leadership, perhaps through his marriage. Rather than being shocked at God's destruction of Sodom, we ought really to marvel at his mercy in delivering Lot and his daughters out of the city.

God sent two angels to warn Lot about the impending disaster and to command him to leave the city.

> With the coming of dawn, the angels urged Lot, say-
> ing, "Hurry! Take your wife and your two daughters
> who are here, or you will be swept away when the city
> is punished." When he hesitated, the men grasped his
> hand and the hands of his wife and of his two daugh-
> ters and led them safely out of the city, for the LORD
> was merciful to them. As soon as they had brought
> them out, one of them said, "Flee for your lives! Don't
> look back, and don't stop anywhere in the plain! Flee
> to the mountains or you will be swept away!" (Gen.
> 19:15–17)

There were three commands: (1) Hurry. (2) Get far
from the area, all the way to the mountains. (3) Don't
look back. Lot failed on all three counts. Instead of
responding with grateful and hasty obedience, the
family seemed indecisive about leaving Sodom, and
even when they did, Lot whined until the Lord agreed
to let them flee only as far as Zoar, a little town in the
plain. And Lot's wife did look back and was turned to a
pillar of salt. There is nothing more than half-hearted
compliance in these behaviors, a far cry from the deep
faith response attained by Lot's Aunt Sarah and Uncle
Abraham.

In spite of her depraved environment and her lack of
spiritual leadership from her husband, it is important
to notice that Lot's wife was still held strictly accountable for her individual act of disobedience. Have you
ever defended your actions with excuses like, "It's not
my fault. I was brought up this way"; or "My husband
should have done thus and so, then I wouldn't be in
this mess"? Whenever we are tempted to blame other

people or circumstances for our troubles, we should remember Lot's wife.

Why did she look back? Clearly, she disobeyed God's express command, but her attitude does not seem to be one of defiance. It was not "I can if I want to" so much as "I just can't help myself." She was simply ... to resist one last look at her home town. We ... both good and bad excuses for her ...:

1. She was lovingly concerned for the remainder of ... family left behind in Sodom.
2. She was simply curious to see the destruction God ... promised.
3. He ... It was too caught up in her possessions and ... style left behind.
4. She ... afraid of the future, and was trying to cling ... the familiar past as long as she could.

Concerned, ... ious, caught up, or clinging—whatever her reasons, nothing could justify her disobedience. The fact remains that she disobeyed God's specific orders and reaped an instantaneous, irreversible consequence. Each of us should learn that our actions cannot be rationalized or retracted without paying a permanent price.

In 1 Samuel 16:7 we read, "The LORD seeth not as man seeth; for man looketh on the outward appearance, but the LORD looketh on the heart" (KJV). The same thought is expressed more strongly in Hebrews 4:12–13:

> The word of God is living and active. Sharper than any double-edged sword, it penetrates even to dividing soul and spirit, joints and marrow; it judges the thoughts and attitudes of the heart. Nothing in all creation is hidden from God's sight. Everything is uncovered and laid bare before the eyes of him to whom we must give account.

God's penetrating judgment at once spares us and condemns us, since our hearts are indeed laid bare before him. There is *no* excuse for sin. Christ used the example of Lot's wife in the context of a solemn warning of impending judgment (Luke 17:28-33). When that day of judgment comes, will you be saved, "but only as one escaping through the flames" (1 Cor. 3:15)? Remember Lot's wife.

God is not capricious. He does not delight in setting traps for his people so that he can invent clever punishments for them, saying, "One glance and I'll zap you into a pillar of salt!" We learned from Eve that we are wrong to conceive of God's rules as an arbitrary exercise of his power. For our benefit he invites each of us to participate in the blessings that follow from obedience. God has reasons for his rules. In his Word he provides directions as to the right and wrong paths for us and tells us the destinations we can expect to reach on each.

Did Lot's wife feel that she didn't need to take God literally, or that it wouldn't matter if she took just one little peek over her shoulder? Perhaps you think that God should be more lovingly lenient over such seemingly trivial details, and that he is entitled to crack down on us only for big sins. But the whole Bible shows us that our behavior in small things reflects the attitudes of our hearts, which are God's ultimate concern. The kings of Israel were sternly warned against collecting pagan wives and horses, yet Solomon, for all his wisdom, lost his kingdom precisely for committing these offenses (compare Deut. 17:14-17 with 1 Kings 10 and 11). His excesses culminated in his turning to follow after other gods, to the point of building altars and sacrificing to those gods. It was not simply a matter of horses and wives, after all, but Solomon's attitude for which he was judged (1 Kings 11:11). One thing led to another, as it does with us. From the beginning God established specific behavioral objectives whereby we can measure our growth toward or our drift away from him. Out of love he desires that we obey him so he can bless us, but he will not hesitate to punish those who disregard his Word, just as a wise parent must reinforce the negative rules as part of establishing a positive relationship with his child.

We can trust God to be absolutely fair, both in clear warning and in judgment. We dare not imagine that we can do as we please and then bargain over big and little sins. God is also absolutely holy. Our response to his detailed commands reveals as much about the attitude of our hearts as our outward compliance with broader biblical principles. We fall into the same sin as Lot's wife whenever we yield to temptation and then claim God's compassion, expecting that he could not really have meant we should have obeyed in *that* area, when we are so faithful in general. However, we can

79

rest securely in the knowledge that *ll* sins are forgiven under the blood of Christ shed for those who trust in him, but we dare not presume that "good old God" does not care what we do or how we treat his Word. He wants us to love *and* obey him (John 14:15–23). We must be willing to give up our past habits and fears and to move forward in faith whenever he directs us, all the way to the mountains. To look back is to refuse to trust God's plan for what lies ahead. Let us beware of becoming "earthen salt," and strive instead to become "the salt of the earth" which Jesus called his disciples (Matt. 5:13). Remember Lot's wife.

## PART THREE

# Women of Subterfuge and Deceit

Rebekah

Rachel

Rebekah and Rachel are two of the most familiar and favorite women of the Bible. Although we sometimes confuse the details of their lives, their names are popular choices for baby girls in every generation. Yet, if we examine their personalities in depth, we discover serious problems with their methods, if not their motives, for gaining their desires.

Rebekah and Rachel were sister and daughter, respectively, of a shady character named Laban, who was not above using any means to make a deal or change a bargain to his own advantage. Both women were also intimately connected with Jacob, whose name figuratively means "deceit."

Rebekah was Jacob's mother. She trained him to scheme to gain his father's blessing and promised him that she would take the consequences of the deceitful act upon herself. Rachel became Jacob's wife, but only after Laban had tricked him into marrying the older daughter first. We wonder if Rachel encouraged Jacob in his trickery, or if she was influenced by him to think first of herself at the expense of others. But however Jacob may have been influenced by his mother and his wife, or have influenced them, both Rebekah and Rachel serve as examples of the outcome of sinful subterfuge.

Rebekah and Rachel were highly intelligent and very beautiful women. The Bible specifically mentions that their husbands loved them (Gen. 24:67, 29:18). But do not think that their many good qualities and spiritual strengths protected them from the possibility of their engaging in sinful practices. God never condones deceit, no matter in how pretty a package it comes. He needs no help to accomplish his purposes, apart from hearts willing to cooperate with him. When we resort to subterfuge, even for supposedly good reasons, we demonstrate that we have more faith in our own stratagems than in God's promises and plans. Pride and discontent were at the root of Rebekah's and Rachel's deceit. Their stories serve more as warnings than as positive models for us, and they challenge us to examine our own hearts, to confess, and to be cleansed from anything that would keep us from an honest relationship with our holy God and with our fellow human beings.

# 6

## Rebekah

### Primary Scripture Reading

Genesis 24–28

### Supplementary References

Genesis 12, 20, 29, 31,
  33, 36, 49
Luke 12:48
2 Timothy 1:12

### Questions for Study and Discussion

**1.** Rebekah was God's answer to a servant's prayer to find a wife for Isaac. List several good qualities of Rebekah's character indicated or implied in Genesis 24.

**2.** Why did Rebekah turn to God (Gen. 25)? How would his prophecy have comforted her? How might it also have caused confusion? How did God keep his promises to Rebekah concerning the future of her twins?

**3.** Why did Isaac favor Esau, while Rebekah preferred Jacob? What effects did these choices have on their household? When is differential treatment of children outright favoritism, and when does it result from parents' sensitivity to individual gifts and needs? Are there ways in which favoritism affected you as a child or as a parent? What might you do to overcome its negative impact on your family?

**4.** List Rebekah's words and actions recorded in Genesis 27. To what extent was she obeying God? How could her outward behavior have been more consistent with her faith?

**5.** What were the immediate and the long-range consequences of Rebekah's actions? Were there any benefits? What other means could God have used to fulfill his promises, without her interference?

**6.** Why, do you think, did Rebekah resort to subterfuge? Have you ever indulged in intrigue or been drawn into deceit? Describe an experience in which you used dishonest methods to accomplish a godly purpose, or when such methods were used in your behalf. Does having good motives sometimes encourage deceitfulness? When do the ends justify the means for a Christian?

**7.** What positive challenge do you receive from Rebekah's story? What comfort? How did God overrule events to accomplish his will for her family? How is he working in your life to keep his promises, in spite of human obstacles to the fulfillment of his will?

Rebekah seemed to have everything going for her when Abraham's servant prayed and then saw her at the well. Beauty, grace, hospitality, courage, and sensitivity were all evident when she responded to God's call to leave her family and become Isaac's wife. Twenty years later, God answered Isaac's prayer in her behalf, and Rebekah conceived twins. When she turned to God for understanding, he gave her a clear promise:

Two nations are in your womb, and two peoples from within you will be separated; one people will be stronger than the other, and the older will serve the younger (Gen. 25:23).

Unfortunately, this propitious beginning seems all but lost when, two chapters later, we meet Rebekah scheming to get Isaac's blessing for Jacob. How could she have become so domineering? Before we look for possible causes of Rebekah's deceit, which may be warning signals for us today, let us first examine the sequence of events in Genesis 27 and their consequences.

## Sequence

Genesis 27 records a series of conversations between pairs of characters, as follows:

| | |
|---|---|
| Isaac and Esau | Genesis 27:1–2 |
| Rebekah and Jacob | Genesis 27:5–17 |
| Jacob and Isaac | Genesis 27:18–29 |
| Isaac and Esau | Genesis 27:30–41 |
| Rebekah and Jacob | Genesis 27:42–45 |
| Rebekah and Isaac | Genesis 27:46 |
| Isaac and Jacob | Genesis 28:1–5 |

This pairing reflects the division that existed within the family. No one ever suggested a council of all the members to work out their desires and differences. The action was held together instead by Rebekah

85

alone. She overheard, then engineered, then listened again. She used her quick wit and ability, first to secure for Jacob his father's blessing and then to protect him from his brother's sworn vengeance. Nerves of steel kept her on the alert for opportunities, which she seized and pushed through to success. Afterward she did not relax with her triumph, but was ready once more to receive the report of Esau's secret determination to kill Jacob, and to send Jacob away to safety. Not satisfied with her initial deception concerning the blessing, she used the excuse of her displeasure with Esau's wives to persuade Isaac to send Jacob to Laban with his blessing.

Rebekah seemed to enjoy taking matters into her own hands. For her, intrigue was more interesting than integrity. Notice her direct involvement: *she* listened to Isaac's conversation with Esau. *She* summoned Jacob and insisted that he obey her orders. *She* offered to take the curse upon herself if Isaac discovered their trick. *She* did the cooking and baking. *She* stole Esau's clothes and put them on Jacob, along with the goatskin pieces for his hands and neck. We can imagine her getting Jacob all decked out, overruling his weak protests, and then shaking a stern finger at him and saying, "After all the trouble *I've* gone to for you, you'd better not blow it now! Lie, steal, cheat, but whatever you do, *get that blessing!*" A charming mother! Nor would she hesitate to listen through the tent wall to catch every word of the crucial conversation between Jacob and Isaac; possibly she gestured or whispered cues to guarantee that nothing would go wrong with her scheme. She would surely have subscribed to the notion that "the best way to get a thing done right is to do it yourself."

Later Rebekah took command again, receiving the news about Esau's anger, ordering Jacob to flee to her brother Laban, and manipulating her husband to endorse her new plan. The only thing that Rebekah did *not* do in this chapter was to recognize the sinfulness of her schemes or to take any responsibility for the trouble *she* had caused. She even said to Jacob, "When your brother is no longer angry with you and forgets what *you* did to him, I'll send word for you to come back from there" (Gen. 27:45).

This picture of Rebekah's overbearing personality may speak to many of us. Are we so set on accomplishing our own purposes that we become blind and deaf to right and reason, whether they come from our own consciences, from those we claim to be trying to help, or as God's warnings?

We cannot excuse Jacob for so readily falling in line with his mother's devious methods. He was forty years old by this time, and should have been wise enough to know God's ways and responsible enough to act in accordance with his will. It is true that Rebekah was not a woman one could easily challenge or hope to swerve from her determined course. Still, the choice to cooperate with her was Jacob's. The only concern he expressed was the fear of getting caught and being cursed.

## Consequences

Rebekah is not mentioned again until Genesis 49:31, where her burial with Isaac is recorded, although her death must have occurred some time earlier. She was never able to summon Jacob back from her brother's house, and she never saw him or his wives or children, so far as we know. This must have been deeply disappointing to her. Although Jacob was officially reconciled to his brother, we know that God fulfilled his promise to Rebekah by establishing two very distinct nations from her offspring. If we follow the histories of Edom, Esau's descendants, and Israel, Jacob's descendants, we can see the rivalry continuing through the centuries down to the present.

Jacob also suffered because of his participation in his mother's plot to wrench Isaac's blessing by means of deceit. After fleeing from his home, he spent more than twenty years with his uncle Laban, at whose hands he experienced many treacheries similar to the one his mother had engineered in his behalf. His wives and children indulged in bitter rivalries, which culminated in the sale into slavery of his favorite son. Ultimately, the whole family joined Joseph in Egypt, a move that ended in the enslavement of the entire nation of Israel for 400 years. Subterfuge and deceit were practiced again and again throughout the Book of Genesis and beyond, even after God delivered his people and gave them his law of truth.

## Precedents

"Oh, what a tangled web we weave, when first we practice to deceive!" (Sir Walter Scott: "The Lay of the Last Minstrel"). Rebekah's life story proves the truth and the sadness of Scott's observation, as we have traced the sequence of her deceit and its consequences for herself and her family. But we have not yet answered the question. She had agreed to marry Isaac on the basis of God's answer to a servant's prayer. God had given her a special promise concerning her twins before they were born. Why did she not rest, secure in his omnipotence to fulfill what he had promised in her life? Three unhappy possibilities may help us to understand Rebekah, as well as ourselves, and to avoid the inclination to deceive when it arises.

First, Rebekah lived among poor models from which to learn honesty. Her brother Laban's full bag of dirty tricks showed up when Jacob came to live and deal with him, but we may suppose that, for whatever cultural or psychological reasons, both brother and sister shared the viewpoint that any tactic is valid that gains an advantage over a vulnerable adversary. In her new home, also, Rebekah saw that neither Abraham nor Isaac was above resorting to deception, repeatedly trying to pass off their wives as their sisters to protect their own lives. The attitude that any behavior is permissible as long as one is not caught seems to have been as popular in ancient times as it is today. As Rebekah looked around her and observed the significant men in her life resorting to subterfuge out of fear or greed, she may have excused her own behavior on the grounds that she, at least, had better motives in mind.

Her better motive is a second possible explanation for Rebekah's scheming. Perhaps she was willing to go to any extremes in order to secure for Jacob the blessing she was sure God had promised. Genesis 25:27–28 describes the preference of each parent for one of the twins:

> The boys grew up, and Esau became a skillful hunter, a man of the open country, while Jacob was a quiet man, staying among the tents. Isaac, who had a taste for wild game, loved Esau, but Rebekah loved Jacob.

This is not really a better motive.

Here is poison also found in our own day—favoritism toward a particular child by a selfish parent. Isaac was a meek man, but he admired his burly outdoorsman son because he enjoyed the fresh game Esau was able to put on his table. "Opposites attract," we say, especially when the appetite is served. Another adage, "Like attracts like," helps us understand Rebekah's love for Jacob, who was content to be a busy homebody like herself, staying among the tents and sharing her interests and ideas. Her spirit of ambition may also have led her to prefer Jacob simply because God had said that "the older will serve the younger." Although we usually think of twins as being born simultaneously, the chronological priority of Esau is repeatedly affirmed in Genesis 27. Rebekah would surely have wanted to be on the side of the winner.

We have seen the bitter fruit of this favoritism in the rivalry that erupted between the boys concerning both the birthright and the blessing. Esau's third marriage, to the daughter of Ishmael, was also a pitiful reaction to his perceived differential treatment.

Unfortunately, Jacob seemed to gain no positive insights from his experiences. If he did, he was powerless to create an atmosphere of greater equality and harmony among his wives and children. Sibling jealousy toward his favorite son Joseph was the instigating factor that ultimately led to the family's departure for Egypt, as we have noted.

Be honest. Do you favor one of your children over the others, for whatever reasons of affinity or contrast? Would you now contemplate the tragic consequences that accompanied such family–fracturing alliances in Rebekah's life? Ask God to give you his sense of balance and harmony to appreciate every individual in your household for the special gifts he has bestowed, and for the special purposes he has intended.

We can delve into Rebekah's background for yet a third possible explanation for her deceitful behavior. Why, when she had received a clear promise from God, did Rebekah resort to subterfuge and rely on her own abilities to scheme in order to achieve what had been promised? Simply because she trusted more in her own abilities than in God who made the promise. At the beginning of our study, we recognized what a gifted individual Rebekah was. We may say teasingly, "It's hard to be humble when you're perfect." But Rebekah lived under the real burden of her many talents. If they were from God, should she not exercise them to the fullest capacity on his behalf? Had he not endowed her so that she could help him fulfill his will for her sons?

A successful businessman in the Middle West once boasted to a gifted young artist, "I've arranged things so that you can attend either Harvard or Princeton, whichever you prefer."

91

"How did you manage that?"

"It was easy. I just told Princeton that you wanted to go to Harvard, and I told Harvard that you wanted to go to Princeton. Now they are both eager to have you!" Obviously, there was little expectation that the young man's personal credentials or God's own subtle arrangements for his college career would have any bearing on the decision. Mr. X felt that *he* had done all the arranging, and he was clearly delighted with his own important role in the intrigue.

Rebekah was rather like this businessman, superbly confident of her ability and indispensability. Her subterfuge was a manifestation of her pride. Though she may have appeared sincerely concerned for Jacob's future, she was actually more preoccupied with her own power in the present. Her priorities became skewed; success was more important and more intoxicating than the simple truth.

Jesus said, "For unto whomsoever much is given, of him shall be much required" (Luke 12:48, KJV). We might add the thought, "She to whom much is given is accountable for whose glory she uses it." Deceit can be a manifestation of conceit. Whether we are trying to conceal what we are or to portray ourselves as something we are not, we must recognize the interplay of our past, our preferences, our priorities, and our pride. Subterfuge is sin, and it inevitably leads to more sin.

If Rebekah's example prods us onto a truer path in our own walk with God, then her sad story will have served a happy purpose. When we comprehend that our all-knowing, all-powerful God is fully "able to keep that which I have committed unto Him" (2 Tim. 1:12, KJV), and to accomplish his will in our lives and the lives of our children, without our manipulations, then we can cooperate more patiently and confidently—even joyfully—with his methods, and receive his blessings.

# 7

## Rachel

### Primary Scripture Reading

Genesis 29–31

### Supplementary References

Genesis 32–35, 37, 45–46
Psalm 42
John 4:13–14
Philippians 4:10–13

### Questions for Study and Discussion

**1.** At the time Jacob met Rachel, what aspects of her personality and home situation did he consider to be blessings? Do you think Rachel viewed herself and her life as blessed? Write down some of your blessings. Are there other blessings you need or want? Would people near you list contentment as one of your attributes?

**2.** Explain the unusual circumstances surrounding Rachel's intended and actual marriage to Jacob. Is there any way Rachel could have improved on or made the best of her situation?

**3.** Which of Laban's character traits and behaviors did Rachel adopt? What aspects of your background do you think help to either explain or excuse your behavior? How can you overcome the power of your past?

**4.** Find the meanings of the names Rachel chose for her sons and the sons of her maidservant. How do they reveal her attitudes toward her husband and sister, as well as toward God?

**5.** Rachel seemed dissatisfied in spite of her blessings, while her sister Leah found a measure of contentment in spite of hardship. Are you restless, or are you resting in the providence of God? Write down some promises of God found in Scripture that might offer encouragement for your situation, and memorize them.

**6.** Why did Rachel steal Laban's household gods? What did she hope to gain? Do you think she or her family benefited from her action? How did she feel about her share of Laban's inheritance? What is your spiritual inheritance in Christ? Are you sure of receiving it?

**7.** Rachel died in childbirth (Gen. 35). Do you find any personality development or spiritual growth through the course of her life? Why did Jacob change the baby's name to Benjamin? Why, do you think, was Rachel not buried in the cave at Machpelah (where Sarah and Abraham were buried, and where Isaac, Rebekah, Leah, and Jacob were later buried)? Was Jacob's monument to her in any way an honor? How does Rachel's example challenge you?

Every spring during the Feast of Passover, Jews celebrate with symbols and songs the history of God's deliverance of his people from Egypt and the hope of future blessing. In one traditional song each verse adds to the record of God's work, followed by a chorus consisting of repetitions of the single word *Dayenu,* which means, "It would have been enough," or "We should have been satisfied." Here is a sample:

> Had he supplied our desert needs
> and not fed us with manna,
> Dayenu, Dayenu, Dayenu.

> Had he brought us to Mount Sinai
> and not given us the Torah,
> Dayenu, Dayenu, Dayenu.

> Had he given us the Torah
> and not led us to the land of Israel,
> Dayenu, Dayenu, Dayenu.

> Had he led us to Israel
> and not built for us the temple,
> Dayenu, Dayenu, Dayenu.

Would any of these intermediate blessings really have been enough? On the one hand, they would not, because God still had more to give. But are we ever as satisfied with God's great goodness as we ought to be? We can never earn the least of his favors, yet do we not find ourselves continually wanting more, more, more? Even as we rejoice in Christ's words, "Whoever drinks the water I give him will never thirst" (John 4:14), we fail to pause in our guzzling long enough to express our gratitude. We may quote Psalm 42:2; "My soul thirsts for God, for the living God;" but too often we desire his presents more than his presence.

We don't usually think of simple discontent as a precursor or a manifestation of dishonesty, but it may actually be an early warning symptom of deeper trouble ahead. In Rachel's story, the elements that caused her early dissatisfaction were never dealt with in a positive way. They festered beneath the surface, sometimes flashing hot or bubbling up unexpectedly, until they finally erupted as the full-blown sins of stealing and lying. Why would such a lovely and much-loved lady commit such crimes? As we trace her relationships with her husband, her sister, her children, and her father, we may discover insights useful to our understanding both of her character and of our own patterns of dealing with resentment.

## Husband

When Jacob fled from the wrath of his brother Esau, he followed his mother's advice and went to Haran in search of his uncle Laban. First he found Rachel, a shepherdess, and daughter of Laban. Jacob identified himself as her cousin, kissed her, and wept aloud. Rachel was "lovely in form, and beautiful," and Jacob soon was in love with her. He offered to work for Laban to earn Rachel as his bride.

> So Jacob served seven years to get Rachel, but they seemed like only a few days to him because of his love for her (Gen. 29:20).

On the wedding night, however, the crafty Laban put his older daughter Leah into the marriage bed. Jacob was livid, but there was nothing to be done but to fulfill Leah's bridal week and then marry Rachel.

Jacob lay with Rachel also, and he loved Rachel more than Leah. And he worked for Laban another seven years (Gen. 29:30).

Later, in the wake of the sisters' competition over childbearing, two maidservants were elevated to wife status as well, but Rachel was always best-beloved. We see this in the care with which Jacob protected her by placing her with her son at the end of the caravan when he met Esau again after twenty years (Gen. 33:1–3). Years later, Jacob's preference for Rachel's children, Joseph and Benjamin, was painfully obvious to his other ten sons (Gen. 37:3, 45:18–29). Unfortunately, the only person who failed to recognize this supreme love and to rest in it was Rachel herself.

God's gifts of love, or beauty, or intelligence, can only reach their full potential for his glory when they are acknowledged and received by the individual on whom they are bestowed. The extent to which these gifts are developed depends largely on the person's attitude and response to them. In the same way, a woman may be loved by a man, but she will radiate that love only to the degree that she chooses to receive and rest in it. Rachel was more beautiful and more beloved than her weak-eyed sister, yet Leah learned to find peace through focusing on God's care in the midst of her difficult circumstances. Neither God's blessing of physical beauty nor Jacob's love was enough for Rachel.

### Sister

To an unusual degree Rachel's relationship with her sister strongly affected her marriage relationship, since Leah also happened to be married to Rachel's husband.

> When Rachel saw that she was not bearing Jacob any children, she became jealous of her sister. So she said to Jacob, "Give me children, or I'll die" (Gen. 30:11).

Thus began the intense competition between the two women over their rights to Jacob's sexual attention. First, Rachel insisted that Jacob sleep with her maid Bilhah so that she could build a family through her servant. Two sons were born. When Leah stopped bearing children of her own, she gave her maid Zilpah to Jacob. Two more sons were added. Rachel was far from satisfied, her jealousy far from soothed.

The following exchange indicates the tense atmosphere that must have pervaded the household during the first thirteen years of this multiple marriage:

> During wheat harvest, Reuben went out into the fields and found some mandrake plants, which he brought to his mother Leah. Rachel said to Leah, "Please give me some of your son's mandrakes." But she said to her, "Wasn't it enough that you took away my husband? Will you take my son's mandrakes too?" "Very well," Rachel said, "he can sleep with you tonight in return for your son's mandrakes." So when Jacob came in from the fields that evening, Leah went out to meet him. "You must sleep with me," she said, "I have hired you with my son's mandrakes." So he slept with her that night (Gen. 30:14–16).

We may be surprised to see in this passage Jacob's abdication of his own authority over the household in the face of these sparring sisters. We see Leah's readiness to drive a hard but petty bargain when she had the opportunity. But we also see the extent to which Rachel jealously guarded her territorial claim to Jacob against her sister. She was not the older sister, nor the first wife, but she was clearly the more dominant woman. Though she granted her a night with Jacob in exchange for the mandrakes, Rachel would have had to answer no to Leah's question, "Wasn't it enough that you took away my husband?" Discontent continued to smolder within her. Nothing was enough.

## Children

For thirteen years Rachel was barren. The social stigma attached to women without children was acute in her day. Rachel must have suffered terribly whenever Leah, Bilhah, and Zilpah became pregnant (eleven times, counting the one for Dinah) while she remained childless. She vented her frustration on her husband, though it was clearly not his fault, and he would have none of it. "Jacob became angry with her and said, 'Am I in the place of God, who has kept you from having children?'" (Gen. 30:2).

Incidentally, God's participation in the miracle of life is especially evident in these chapters. Notice Genesis 29:31: "When the LORD saw that Leah was not loved, he opened her womb, but Rachel was barren." Chapter 30:17 states: "God listened to Leah, and she became pregnant and bore Jacob a fifth son." Finally, in verse

22 we read, "Then God remembered Rachel; he listened to her and opened her womb."

Rachel had to wait a long time for God to bless her in this way. Perhaps he was waiting to see whether her attitude might improve. It did not. Rachel steadfastly refused to be satisfied with her circumstances. She persisted in looking at the negative side of her situation.

When Rachel's maid bore Jacob a son in her name,

> Rachel said, "God has vindicated me; he has listened to my plea and given me a son." Because of this she named him Dan (Gen. 30:6).

Dan means "God has vindicated." Rachel recognized that God had listened to her prayers, but she chose to regard his gift as vindication, her "just due" to make up for her past suffering, rather than as his provision for her out of his love.

When Bilhah's second son was born,

> Rachel said, "I have had a great struggle with my sister, and I have won." So she named him Naphtali (Gen. 30:8).

Naphtali means "my struggle." Again she considered the child as a sign of victory over her sister in compensation for her unhappiness.

Even the birth of Rachel's own son did not fully satisfy her. She merely said,

"God has taken away my disgrace." She named him Joseph, and said, "May the LORD add to me another son" (Gen. 30:23–24).

One son was not enough. Nothing was enough.

Many years passed. Jacob built up his herds and left Laban (Gen. 31). He was reconciled to his brother Esau (Gen. 32–33). He settled in Shechem, where his elder sons killed all the men and plundered the city in revenge for the violation of their sister (Gen. 34). God told Jacob to move his family to Bethel, where he renewed his covenant.

Then they moved on from Bethel. While they were still some distance from Ephrath, Rachel began to give birth and had great difficulty. And as she was having great difficulty in childbirth, the midwife said to her, "Don't be afraid, for you have another son." As she breathed her last—for she was dying—she named her son Ben-Oni. But his father named him Benjamin (Gen. 35:16–18).

Here Rachel aptly expressed her perception of her whole life and revealed her capacity for self-pity when she named her baby "son of my trouble." Her devoted husband overruled her choice and gave him the name that means "son of my right hand," suggesting not only that he would treasure this son in a special way, but also that Rachel had been like a right hand to him. How sad that we cannot find more evidence of this positive, supportive quality of her character recorded in Scripture. When Rachel died, Jacob honored her tomb with a pillar, and to this day the site remains an important landmark in Bethlehem. In her lifetime, however, it seems that all Rachel constructed was a monument to her own misery.

There is a story about a wealthy New Englander who went to the bank near closing time and insisted on withdrawing $10,000 in small denominations. He carefully counted the $10 bills. The line behind him grew restless as he meticulously counted the $5 bills. The tellers became impatient as he painstakingly counted the $1 bills.

"Well," snapped the manager, "is it all there?"

"It's all here," replied the gentleman, "just barely."

How ready are you to recognize, receive, and rest in God's goodness toward you? Do you find it so abundant that your cup overflows with his blessings? Or is it merely enough—barely sufficient to satisfy your needs and desires? Or do you continue to compare yourself to others whom you perceive to be more fortunate, and to complain about the things you do not have? Do you concentrate on the unfilled portion of the cup, and in so doing fail to appreciate all that God has provided?

## Father

Laban was a crafty character. Over the course of twenty years he switched Jacob's wives, wages, and livestock for his own advantage. He was devious and deceitful. It was probably his philosophy that Rachel imitated in her fruitless quest for fulfillment, for she, too, was always looking to protect or enhance her own position by means of the next sneaky maneuver. Although she resembled her father in this way, Rachel had little respect for him. The only subject about which she seemed to agree with her sister Leah was that their father had cheated them. Jacob told his wives that he had "noticed that Laban's attitude toward him was not what it had been" (Gen. 31:2), and that God had directed him to return to the land of his fathers.

Then Rachel and Leah replied, "Do we still have any share in the inheritance of our father's estate? Does he not regard us as foreigners? Not only has he sold us, but he has used up what was paid for us. Surely all the wealth that God took away from our father belongs to us and our children. So do whatever God has told you" (Gen. 31:14–16).

But Rachel went one step farther than her sister. "When Laban had gone to shear his sheep, Rachel stole her father's household gods" (Gen. 31:19). Furthermore, "Jacob did not know that Rachel had stolen the gods" (Gen. 31:32). He angrily insisted that Laban search among his goods, and he promised to put to death anyone found to have taken them.

So Laban went into Jacob's tent and into Leah's tent and into the tent of the two maidservants, but he found nothing. After he came out of Leah's tent, he entered Rachel's tent. Now Rachel had taken the household gods and put them inside her camel's saddle and was sitting on them. Laban searched through everything in the tent but found nothing. Rachel said to her father, "Don't be angry, my lord, that I cannot stand up in your presence; I'm having my period." So he searched but could not find the household gods (Gen. 31:33–35).

Two facts pertaining to the culture of that time should be pointed out before we make any judgments about this incident. First, the household gods represented tokens of inheritance more than symbols of idolatry. Whoever possessed them could lay claim to a man's property after his death. Second, as God later spelled out for the Israelites, it was considered an act of uncleanness to touch either a menstruating woman or anything on which she sat (Lev. 15:19–23). God intended this law as a hygienic protection, but Rachel counted on the same principle to cover her theft. As she expected, Laban did not press his search.

Because she had an older sister and several brothers, Rachel must have realized that she had no legitimate claim to her father's property, regardless of who possessed his household gods. Her act was spontaneous, motivated more by a desire to retaliate against her family than out of any deliberate plan to gain lasting benefit for herself. The combination of stealing and lying in this incident was simply another expression of her accumulating dissatisfactions. The household gods were never redeemed; in fact, Jacob later demanded their burial (Gen. 35).

What alternative did Rachel have? How can people resolve their feelings of resentment in productive, permanent ways? Leah's life demonstrates a determination to face the facts, confess her feelings, and focus on the Lord as a reliable source of fulfillment in every circumstance. Jacob likewise learned to accept his difficult situation by finding evidence of God's blessing even in the midst of hardship (Gen. 31:5,7,9). But Rachel refused to be comforted by the blessings God had so faithfully provided. She chose instead to brood over her father's treachery, her sister's fecundity, her husband's conflicting duties, and her own failure to bear children. Rather than making the best of her current circumstances, she was haunted by the past and her unfulfilled dream of what could have been; perhaps she even began to wallow in her discontent. She insisted on trying to manipulate the future.

To be lovely and much loved was not enough for Rachel. Rather than overcoming her circumstances, she succumbed to bitterness. Rather than resting, she was restless. Nothing was enough; she wanted more.

Are you, like Rachel, headed downhill on a course of dissatisfaction that may end in dishonesty and deceit, or in disappointment and despair? Accept God's love. Believe that in every trial he desires to draw you closer to himself, to sustain you with his sufficiency until you realize that he is indeed "enough." Then you can join the refrain of Psalm 118, also sung during the Passover celebration: "Give thanks to the LORD, for he is good. His love endures forever."

Jesus said,

Everyone who drinks this water will be thirsty again, but whoever drinks the water I give him will never thirst. Indeed, the water I give him will become in him a spring of water welling up to eternal life (John 4:13–14).

107

Have you found Christ to be your thirst quencher, your resting place? Is his love, his sacrifice, enough for you?

> My faith has found a resting place,
> Not in device nor creed;
> I trust the everliving one,
> His wounds for me shall plead.
>
> I need no other argument,
> I need no other plea,
> It is enough that Jesus died,
> And that he died for me.
>
> Enough for me that Jesus saves,
> That ends my fear and doubt;
> A sinful soul I come to him,
> He'll never cast me out.
>
> I need no other argument,
> I need no other plea,
> It is enough that Jesus died,
> And that he died for me.

> Liddie H. Edmunds, 1891

## PART FOUR

# Women with a Message

Deborah

Huldah

Miriam

Abigail

Naaman's Maid

Naomi

What are the limits to which a woman can or should rise in her society? Who determines those limits and imposes them? What is God's view of a woman's place? Has his model woman changed from Old Testament to New Testament to modern times? The six women with a message in the final section of this book offer a broad spectrum of possibilities, from a national leader to a housewife to a servant girl, and from very old to very young. Some of the women moved individuals, others entire nations with their words. One needed boldness from God to risk speaking up at all, another needed rebuke to keep from speaking outside of his will. More than mere mouthpieces, they each had unique gifts and personalities that needed molding and refining to make them suitable vessels for God's purpose at a given moment. While using them to reach others God also taught them valuable lessons of personal faith.

Even though we find encouragement in these examples of "total women," we must not try to remove them totally from the biblical and cultural contexts in which they lived and led, nor must we impose our own biases onto them. The direction of impact should be from the Scriptures to our own lives, not the other way around. Rather than judging their characters by our standards, we should let them suggest ways for us to express messages of truth and joy in the Lord and to help us find what, when, and how God wants us to speak for him.

# 8

## Deborah

### Primary Scripture Reading

Judges 4–5

### Supplementary References

Deuteronomy 18:15–22
1 Corinthians 11:3–12
1 Timothy 2:11–12

### Questions for Study and Discussion

**1.** How is Deborah described in Judges 4? In what ways was she similar to the judges before and after her? How was she unique?

**2.** What are the criteria for a true prophet listed in Deuteronomy 18:15–22? Did Deborah satisfy the conditions? How effectively do you interpret God's message to others?

**3.** How was Deborah associated with Lapidoth? With Barak? How well, do you think, did she distinguish between her domestic and her professional life? Is this issue an area of conflict or confusion for you?

**4.** How much authority did Deborah the judge have over Israel as a nation and over Barak as an individual? What was the source of her authority and how did she use it? Did she take more authority than she should have, or use it in a wrong way?

**5.** Exactly what did Deborah say to Barak? How did her words serve either to encourage or to rebuke him? What did she do to reinforce her instructions? How do you support others physically as well as spiritually?

**6.** What do 1 Timothy 2:11–12 and 1 Corinthians 11:3–12 say about the role of women? Does Deborah's example contradict the New Testament model? How can you exercise your spiritual gifts in proper relationship to men in your family, church, and work?

**7.** To whom did Deborah give credit for Israel's victory? Notice the different people, as well as the specific characteristics of God, who receive her praise. Who was cursed in her song? Why? How do you show appreciation to all the participants in your victories?

Though one of the best-known women of the Old Testament, Deborah is probably one of the most controversial. She both supports and contradicts every neat evaluation of her character. Commentators seeking support for their sexist arguments often stumble on her case. Other scholars would feel more comfortable had she been left out of Scripture entirely. What can we learn from Deborah? We must come to her story with an honest and open mind, without trying to twist it to reflect our own biases. Only then may we find God's message to us through the life of this complex woman.

The period of Israel's history recorded in the Book of Judges consists of intervals of peace followed by years of captivity, as God's people turned toward him and then away from him. The particular oppressors and saviors varied, but the pattern was the same for over 300 years. The last sentence of the Book of Judges is an apt summary of that whole period and an appropriate warning for our own time. "In those days there was no king in Israel: every man did that which was right in his own eyes" (Judg. 21:25, KJV). In the middle of this cycle is Deborah, the fourth judge of Israel.

We learn facts about Deborah from Judges 4:4. She was (a) "a prophetess," (b) "wife of Lapidoth," and (c) "leading Israel at that time." The Bible does not mention the juxtaposition of these three roles in regard to any other character. It is this uniqueness that makes Deborah such an important and challenging woman for our study. We shall consider these attributes one at a time.

## Prophetess

A prophetess is a female prophet, "one who is divinely inspired to communicate God's will to his people and to disclose the future to them."[1] There is no doubt that Deborah functioned as a prophetess when she summoned Barak to her, relayed God's command to him to engage Sisera's army in battle, and promised him victory. This was her communication of God's will. She also foretold the future by announcing that Sisera would be killed at the hands of a woman, an

---

1. Merrill F. Unger, *Unger's Bible Dictionary* (Chicago: Moody Press, 1951)

honor denied to Barak in judgment of his weakness. The accuracy of Deborah's predictions proved the validity of her title as prophetess, according to the test prescribed in Deuteronomy 18.

Are you a prophetess? Prophecy is included among the spiritual gifts to the church, described in 1 Corinthians 12 and Romans 12. Though God promises that every believer will receive at least one gift, we may not all be prophetesses in that special sense. Nevertheless, we are all directed to

> Give thanks to the LORD, call on his name; make known among the nations what he has done. Sing to him, sing praise to him; tell of all his wonderful acts (Ps. 105:1–2).

Therefore, we all can be "forth tellers" of God's words and works, and thus prophetesses, proclaimers of his glory, in everything we say and do.

## Wife

Deborah was also the wife of Lapidoth. All that we know about Lapidoth is that he was Deborah's husband. We do not have to assume that he had died by the time Deborah became a prophetess and judge for the nation, which some commentators have proposed. We read that she was his wife, not his widow. It is true that it would have been very unusual, if not unique, for a Hebrew wife to have so much freedom and authority outside her domestic domain as Deborah exhibited. Perhaps it is for this very reason that her story has been preserved for us. Deborah provides a great example of a working wife, a timely model for decisions and relationships in many families.

For economic and personal reasons, many women today are electing to pursue careers outside the home in addition to managing their responsibilities as wives and mothers. How it was decided that Deborah could or should work in behalf of her country as well as her family is not known to us; but *why* the decision was made seems clear enough, and worthy of our notice. Deborah was not looking for a job just to get out of the house. The Bible does not record for us the scene in which God let her know of her calling, as with Moses at the burning bush, but there was obviously no question that God had appointed and enabled her to serve him as prophetess and judge at that time. It was his will, his message, and his righteous judgment that she was to communicate to his people. Neither she, nor Lapidoth, nor Barak, nor the people of Israel seemed inclined to question her position or her performance for the Lord.

A question all working people might consider is whether God has called them to communicate his message in their communities through their work and to live its truth in their homes. Deborah's example encourages us to realize that when God calls us to represent him in the workplace he will honor the message we communicate in his behalf, if we depend on his help.

The same sentence that tells us Deborah was a prophetess and a judge in Israel also says that she was the wife of Lapidoth. All we can glean from this phrase

115

is that here was a man willing to have his wife serve God and the whole nation as well as his own household. He had a part in her ministry by releasing her to represent him, too; he identified his name with hers, and only that connection is preserved for us in Scripture. Have you thanked your family members for appreciating and supporting your involvement in the activities, friendships, and needs that call you away from home?

## Judge

Judges 4:5 explains what it meant for Deborah to be judge or leader in Israel:

> She held court under the Palm of Deborah between Ramah and Bethel in the hill country of Ephraim, and the Israelites came to her to have their disputes decided.

The fact that the palm tree was named for her indicates the esteem in which she was held by the entire nation. It also shows us that Deborah was accessible; the Israelites knew that they could find her under or near her palm, just as today we expect to find a doctor or lawyer in the office that bears her name over the door. Deborah must have been an effective judge; the people came to her for judgment and apparently went away satisfied with her interpretation of the law and application of God's justice.

We don't know exactly how long Deborah judged in this way before she stepped forward to superintend

Barak's victory over Sisera's army, or how long she ruled afterwards. Judges 5:31 tells us that the land had peace forty years, but we cannot determine whether this figure represented the full period of Deborah's leadership or only the amount of time that elapsed before the LORD delivered the Israelites into the hands of the Midianites (Judg. 6). In any case, forty years of peace seems to have been a common figure among the judges in Israel. The same length of time is indicated following the deliverances by the two previous judges, Othniel and Gideon. Later, Eli also judged forty years. Deborah's administration was thus typical of her time. She had neither the longest nor the shortest tenure; she was neither the greatest nor the least significant. Nothing unusual occurred because she was a woman, and it is even possible that there were other female leaders during this period whose names were not included in the Scripture record. The inclusion of Deborah's administration in Judges 4 and 5 seems not so much to demonstrate a remarkable occurrence as to state a simple fact. We cannot ignore her existence; neither should we make too much of her account. Deborah was leading Israel at that time.

Perhaps God has called some of us to be leaders at this time. What can we learn from the record of Deborah's style of leadership that can help us serve God effectively as leaders? The main difficulty we encounter in trying to reconcile Deborah's role with our own is that several passages in the New Testament seem to insist that a woman should never take a position of leadership over a man. Paul states:

A woman should learn in quietness and full submission. I do not permit a woman to teach or to have authority over a man; she must be silent (1 Tim. 2:11–12).

In 1 Corinthians 11:3–12 Paul amplifies his view of the relationship of women to men:

Now I want you to realize that the head of every man is Christ, and the head of the woman is man, and the head of Christ is God. . . . And every woman who prays or prophesies with her head uncovered dishonors her head—it is just as though her head were shaved. . . . the woman is the glory of man. For man did not come from woman, but woman from man; neither was man created for woman, but woman for man. . . . the woman ought to have a sign of authority on her head. In the Lord, however, woman is not independent of man, nor is man independent of woman. For as woman came from man, so also man is born of woman. But everything comes from God.

The head of Christ is God, but Christ and God are equal partners with the Holy Spirit in the Trinity. Authority does not necessarily mean superiority. Other verses point out the difference between voluntary submission and forced subjection of women.

Is there a contradiction between mutual dependence and male dominance in interpersonal relationships? Would Paul have argued that Deborah was out of line in exercising authority over Barak and all Israel? Was it acceptable for her but unthinkable for modern women to have such influence? If the guidelines have changed, why? These questions are most provocative, if not explosive, in the church today. Our own answers will depend on our religious backgrounds, our experiences, and our various interpretations of the texts. The important thing for us is not to sacrifice a faithful reading of Deborah's story for the sake of proving our personal positions.

Exactly how did Deborah behave? We know that Deborah said three things to Barak:

1. "The LORD, the God of Israel, commands you: 'Go, take with you ten thousand men of Naphtali and Zebulun and lead the way to Mount Tabor. I will lure Sisera, the commander of Jabin's army, with his chariots and his troops to the Kishon River and give him into your hands'" (Judg. 4:6–7).
2. "Very well, I will go with you. But because of the way you are going about this, the honor will not be yours, for the LORD will hand Sisera over to a woman" (Judg. 4:9).
3. "Go! This is the day the LORD has given Sisera into your hands. Has not the LORD gone ahead of you?" (Judg. 4:14).

From reading these statements we realize that Deborah's words to Barak were not so much commands challenging his authority as they were revelations urging him to action. Deborah's main concern was to convey God's message and to see his will accomplished. Her second statement was a rebuke to Barak for his cowardice and lack of faith; but her focus was still on his relationship to God, not on his relationship to her. It was Barak's choice to refuse to trust God for the victory over Sisera. God responded directly by taking away from him the honor of killing Sisera.

Deborah was neither an Amazon nor a Joan-of-Arc figure. She relayed God's call and commands to Barak, but never claimed the role of commander-in-chief for herself. She usurped no man's prerogative, but lent Barak her support as she accompanied him to Kedesh. She tried to impress upon him the necessity of dependence on the Lord alone instead of on her strength of character. And the woman who killed Sisera by God's decree was not Deborah, but Jael.

Barak's own abilities are evident in the fact that he promptly mustered ten thousand foot soldiers and successfully led them against Sisera's nine hundred chariots of iron. It was Barak, not Deborah, whose deeds of faith are recognized in Hebrews 11:32–34. "Barak . . . became powerful in battle and routed foreign armies." Partners in ministry on the battlefield. Deborah and Barak used their talents cooperatively rather than competitively. Together they achieved God's purpose of peace. In what ways do we cooperate or compete with others to do God's work in our homes, churches, or offices?

Perhaps we feel that God has not appointed us to particular positions of leadership either outside or within our homes. Most likely we are women who are not specificially prophetesses or judges to our nation or neighborhoods. Even so, God has commissioned each one of us to speak forth his eternal message, his Word, in every circumstance and conversation of our lives. We can express courage and confidence, joy and truth on our personal battlefields. Deborah challenges us to accomplish the routing of foreign armies (personal sins in our lives) by becoming more deeply rooted in God's Word. Personal growth may be a less glamourous task than public government, but it is an equally crucial endeavor.

Deborah obviously had many natural and spiritual gifts. Her greatest strength, however, was her faithfulness to deliver God's message, not her own. Whether under the palm tree, on the battlefield, or in her victory celebration, she focused on his power, not on her own position. In her song, recorded as Judges 5, she combined God's words with her physical presence to encourage Barak; she offered praise to the Lord for his power and people. She recognized individuals and tribes for their contributions to the victory, but her purpose was always to honor God's name.

> When the princes in Israel take the lead,
> When the people willingly offer themselves—
> Praise the LORD!
> Hear this, you kings! Listen, you rulers!
> I will sing to the LORD, I will sing;
> I will make music to the LORD, the God of Israel
> (Judg. 5:2–3).

We do well to contrast Deborah's example with our attitudes after a crisis has passed. How highly do we evaluate our own role, or that of another person, instead of praising God for his help? Do we feel that a timely word or action from us has saved the day, or do we worship the Lord for his perfect timing of all things?

At the same time, we must beware of belittling the importance of our physical support while we emphasize our spiritual resources. We can often encourage our families and friends with a you-can-do-it-in-God's-strength message, and then be physically present during times of battle in their lives. Or do we tend merely to offer pat Scripture verses and then turn our backs, pursuing our own affairs without risking the pain of personal involvement? Deborah pointed Barak to God's power, but she did not withdraw from participating in battle and praising God. It is one thing to pray *for* someone, and something else again to stand *with* him or her in trials and victories.

Before we leave our study of Deborah we should notice another aspect of her leadership ability, namely her response toward Barak's and all Israel's dependence on her. For example, how do we react when someone suggests that we are natural leaders or essential members of committees? Do we think, "Of course you can't do it without me," or "I can't possibly take such an enormous responsibility"? Both responses diminish our effectiveness and attractiveness as leaders. We can discover in Deborah's reaction three clues to handling such invitations.

First, she identified God, not herself, as the true leader. Her message and power came from him. She thus challenged Barak to obey and seek God's will instead of questioning her orders. Second, Deborah shared the responsibilities and the offering of praise. She insisted that Barak act as general of the army. She praised the tribes that sent fighting men to the battle, and extolled Jael's daring and dramatic murder of Sisera. From her we learn the value of the team approach to our projects, as opposed to star performances by us. Third, Deborah took action. Because she led, others followed through to victory. Her energy and confidence, combined with God's clear purpose, were irresistible against Jabin's 900 iron chariots, even in the face of her own people's fear and reluctance to fight. Deborah was neither a selfish nor self-conscious leader of her people. She accepted the abilities and tasks God had appointed to her, and she knew that he would enable her to carry them out. Do we have the same certainty about our work with God?

Far from being irrelevant to Christian women today, Deborah's example is most pertinent and enlightening to us as we strive to apply God's principles to our own lives. Instead of contradiction we find in it confirmation of Paul's view concerning the interdependence of men and women. And Christ taught this:

The kings of the Gentiles lord it over them; and those who exercise authority over them call themselves Benefactors. But you are not to be like that. Instead, the greatest among you should be like the youngest, and the one who rules like the one who serves. For who is greater, the one who is at the table or the one who serves? Is it not the one who is at the table? But I am among you as one who serves. You are those who have stood by me in my trials. And I confer on you a kingdom, just as my Father conferred one on me, so that you may eat and drink at my table in my kingdom and sit on thrones, judging the twelve tribes of Israel (Luke 22:25–30).

Every believer is admonished to yield his or her personal ambitions and abilities in service to all. This attitude glorifies God more than any honors or victories we may win for ourselves. Deborah compels us to examine our own motives and methods, whether we serve in leadership positions or serve under leadership.

# 9

## Huldah

### Primary Scripture Reading

2 Kings 21–23
2 Chronicles 34–35

### Supplementary References

2 Kings 20
Jeremiah 1:1–4
Zephaniah 1:1–2
Galatians 3:26–29

### Questions for Study and Discussion

**1.** Who was king of Judah in Huldah's day, and what was the state of the nation?

**2.** What was found at the temple? Why was it a surprise? Why do you think it was brought to Huldah? What other well-known prophets might have been consulted?

**3.** What was Huldah's response to the request? Whom did she consult? How do you think the role of prophetess might be different today than it was for Huldah? How is it similar?

**4.** Huldah must have been well-known and well-regarded by the priest. What is your reputation in the eyes of your minister? Does anyone seek your advice on spiritual matters? How do you respond?

**5.** What was King Josiah's response to Huldah's prophecy? Did God change his mind as a result of Josiah's actions? How did Judah and Josiah benefit?

**6.** Huldah is remembered in Scripture for a single service to God. How was she prepared prior to God's specific appointment? What distractions do you need to eliminate in order to be better prepared and aware when God calls on you to serve him?

**7.** Josiah heard and responded to God's stern words spoken through Huldah. How much of the straight truth from God do you really want to hear? Are you prepared to respond to his confrontation as well as to receive his consolation? List several reforms God is now prompting you to initiate. How will you begin to accomplish them?

Of all the women named in the Bible, Huldah's name must be one of the least familiar to our ears. Yet she was obviously respected in her own time and was used by God at a critical moment in Judah's history. Her message, and the manner in which she delivered it, challenges each of us to choose and use our words carefully, and in response to the gifts and assignments God has given us.

### Reputation

King Josiah was Judah's last good ruler. He came to the throne at the age of eight, and eventually worked furiously to abolish the idolatry that had polluted the nation for generations. He instituted many social reforms and set about to restore the temple in Jerusalem. During the cleanup process a scroll was discovered, probably a portion of Deuteronomy that had been buried years earlier in some wall or archive of the now-neglected sanctuary. Josiah reacted strongly to the contents of the scroll.

> When the king heard the words of the Book of the Law, he tore his robes. He gave these orders to Hilkiah the priest. . . ."Go and inquire of the LORD for me and for the people and for all Judah about what is written in this book that has been found. Great is the LORD's anger that burns against us because our fathers have not obeyed the words of this book; they have not acted in accordance with all that is written there concerning us." Hilkiah . . . went to speak to the prophetess Huldah, who was the wife of Shallum son of Tikvah, the son of Harhas, keeper of the wardrobe. She lived in Jerusalem, in the Second District (2 Kings 22:11–14).

Verse 14 above contains Huldah's entire biography in the Bible. Like the judge Deborah she is identified both as a prophetess and as a wife. It is her husband's genealogy that is included as the means of locating her in the annals of Judah. But Huldah did not lead Israel as Deborah did. Her prophetic powers must have been widely recognized or she would never have been consulted about the newly-discovered Book of the Law. But Huldah was not a national leader, nor even the only available person to reveal God's Word to his people in her day. The great figures Jeremiah and Zephaniah were both active during Josiah's reign (see

127

Jer. 1:1–4 and Zeph. 1:1–2). Several other capable civil advisors must have served the kingdom as well.

From among such illustrious personalities, why was Huldah selected to be the one through whom Josiah inquired of the Lord concerning the scroll? Surely it was not because she had her nose in all the neighborhood gossip, nor because she advertised herself as a self-appointed expert on every subject, like Lucy in the "Peanuts" cartoon series. Huldah was a prophetess. Her gift and her dedication to know and to speak God's truth were apparent and available. She was neither pushy nor secretive, but simple and straightforward when her services were called upon. She was sought after because she did her job.

Huldah's reputation is important for us to consider if we want to learn how to use the gifts God has given us for our church and community. We, too, must do our jobs. First we must realize what our gifts are; then we must exercise them, not for our own glory but for the glory of God. Huldah must have merited her reputation as a prophetess both by possessing the real gift of prophecy and by practicing it wholeheartedly. We can't be entirely sure what this practice entailed in Huldah's day. In our time the life of a prophetess includes a deep love for the Lord, diligence in prayer, and a strong desire to express the reality of God's presence, power, and purposes to others.

What kind of reputation do you have? Do people come to you because of your free-flowing opinions, or because you are known as a person who inquires of the Lord in close and constant fellowship? Perhaps you are not endowed with the spiritual gift of prophesy in the strict sense of Romans 12. Still, all of God's people are called upon to abide in him in such a way that their lives are consistent with his truth and available for his use (Matt. 5:16).

Huldah's established reputation helped to define her position. We see her functioning within her appointed domain, in cooperation with other people but not in competition with them. The king, the high priest, other royal officials, and other prophets continued to carry out their duties without interference from her. She had no ambition to take over every office, but only the desire to perform her own task. In achieving recognition as a prophetess Huldah also recognized what she was not. How well do we recognize and accept our limitations in regard to the manifold ministries of our churches?

Huldah is named in the Bible for a single communication rendered in service to God and through his power. To us with our complex lives, in which much of our energy is scattered in many directions, she presents a challenge to seek and serve God according to the specific purpose he has for each of us. What does he want us to be and to do for him? What distractions must we eliminate from our lives in order to pursue singlemindedly and successfully the goal of glorifying him in the tasks to which he has appointed us?

## Response

How often in a committee or other meeting do we make suggestions beginning with the phrase, "I think we should . . ."? Or, if a friend comes for comfort or counsel, do we instantly reply, "If I were you, this is what I would do . . . "? Notice the first-person pronouns, focusing on self—*my* opinions and *my* reactions.

When Josiah sent his emissaries to Huldah, she did not respond with her own ideas. She probably did not respond at all, but simply inquired of the Lord as she was asked to do, until she received his answer.

> She said to them, "This is what the LORD, the God of Israel, says: Tell the man who sent you to me, 'This is what the LORD says: I am going to bring disaster on this place and its people, according to everything written in the book the king of Judah has read. Because they have forsaken me and burned incense to other gods and provoked me to anger by all the idols their hands have made, my anger will burn against this place and will not be quenched.' Tell the king of Judah, who sent you to inquire of the LORD, 'This is what the LORD, the God of Israel, says concerning the words you have heard: Because your heart was reponsive and you humbled yourself before the LORD when you heard what I have spoken against this place and its people, that they would become accursed and laid waste, and because you tore your robes and wept in my presence, I have heard you, declares the LORD. Therefore I will gather you to your fathers, and you will be buried in peace. Your eyes will not see all the disaster I am going to bring on this place'" (2 Kings 22:15–20).

Count the number of times Huldah mentioned God's name in the above passage. All of the first-person pronouns quoted are his words, not hers. When Huldah delivered God's message she did not add one word of commentary. Huldah obviously had to be in close communication with God in order to inquire of him and to receive his exact response. Her accurate transmission demonstrated both her faith and her courage. Because she trusted his precision, the combined power of God's wrath and his mercy were clearly relayed through her. She felt no need to soften the blow for the king's ears; though he might not be pleased with the message, he, too, desired and received the straight truth from God.

Here is another good lesson for us. Sometimes God's words are comforting, sometimes confronting. We may do him and our friends a disservice if we attempt to interpret or tone down the full thrust of his message in our efforts to comfort friends whom God is confronting with his truth.

## Results

Huldah's message from God to Josiah was not exactly a promise of deliverance. God's wrath would still be visited on Judah's wickedness. The only consolation for Josiah was that the judgment would be postponed until after his death because of his faith. What were the results of this prophecy? The New International Version gives this chapter heading to 2 Kings 23: "Josiah Renews the Covenant." He had already instituted many reforms and restorations before the discovery of the Book of the Law. Following Huldah's prophecy Josiah led the nation in a great spiritual revival. He summoned all the people, priests, and prophets, and read to them all the words of the scroll.

> The king stood by the pillar and renewed the covenant in the presence of the LORD—to follow the LORD and keep his commands, regulations and decrees with all his heart and all his soul, thus confirming the words of the covenant written in this book. Then all the people pledged themselves to the covenant (2 Kings 23:3).

Josiah redoubled his campaign against idolatry throughout his kingdom and ordered the greatest celebration of the Passover feast ever held in Jerusalem.

> Not since the days of the judges who led Israel, nor throughout the days of the kings of Israel and the kings of Judah, had any such Passover been observed (2 Kings 23:22).

His efforts ranked him as the greatest king in Judah's history.

> Neither before nor after Josiah was there a king like him who turned to the LORD as he did—with all his heart and with all his soul and with all his strength, in accordance with all the Law of Moses (2 Kings 23:25).

Perhaps part of the motivation behind Josiah's devoted leadership was the hope that the prophecy's realization might be lessened or reversed if the people of Judah repented and returned to true worship and obedience of the Lord. Josiah knew that God's grace had already been manifested in this way to the prophet Jonah and to King Hezekiah in Judah's recent past (2 Kings 20). To his credit, Josiah's concern was for his people, not for himself. Although he knew he would be spared, he exerted himself in behalf of the whole nation. Huldah's message stirred him to action, not to complacency or despair. Having done everything he could, Josiah accepted God's judgment, which remained unchanged. "Nevertheless, the LORD did not turn away from the heat of his fierce anger, which burned against Judah" (2 Kings 23:26). But Josiah died years before the destruction of Judah, just as Huldah had said he would.

## Reality and Responsibility

We, too, can profit from the life of this obscure prophetess Huldah. The fact that she is mentioned at all makes a great deal of difference in the way we understand God's selection of his servants throughout history. Because he chose this relatively unknown woman to deliver his message to Josiah, when several highly competent and powerful men were active and available, we should be encouraged regarding the possibility of his appointment of women in any age. God is neither a chauvinist nor a bigot. The inclusion of Huldah's story in Scripture confirms the truth that God does not categorically eliminate anyone from his service, much less from his salvation, on the basis of sex, race, or nationality, but only on the basis of the personal response or lack of faith. Biblical characters such as Huldah show us the balance and depth of

God's revealed attitudes and requirements. He can and does accomplish his will through any and all individuals who will submit themselves to it.

> You are all sons of God through faith in Christ Jesus, for all of you who were baptized into Christ have been clothed with Christ. There is neither Jew nor Greek, slave nor free, male nor female, for you are all one in Christ Jesus. If you belong to Christ, then you are Abraham's seed, and heirs according to the promise (Gal. 3:26–29).

Huldah's name does not appear in a scriptural spotlight. Her role was small but important. If you would be useful to God today, trust him to assign you a task of appropriate size and significance according to his eternal perspective, not as measured by the vanity of men or women. Huldah's humility and honesty made her a clear channel for God's timely message to Josiah.

God uses individuals to testify to his truth through their clear expression of his Word. Such a privilege carries a great responsibility for us to abide in him continually in order to be prepared at the crucial moment of service. Huldah challenges each of us to deepen our communion with the Lord and to concentrate on his appointed tasks, so that the message of our lives transmits his message to others.

# 10

## Miriam

### Primary Scripture Reading

Exodus 2, 15, 18
Numbers 12, 20

### Supplementary References

Psalm 139
Micah 6:4
Mark 4:24–25

### Questions for Study and Discussion

**1.** We may assume the sister of Moses mentioned in Exodus 2 was Miriam. What characteristics do you find in her as a young girl? Compare these with her personality as an old woman, portrayed in Numbers 12. How did she change?

**2.** Miriam was obviously a highly gifted woman. How did she use her gifts throughout her life? What warning concerning your ability to influence people to either praise or defy God do you find in her example?

**3.** What was the source of Miriam's frustration in Numbers 12? What was her motive for complaining? How was Miriam's criticism of Moses also a criticism of God?

**4.** In the same chapter, why did God wait until the situation erupted in a crisis before calling a summit conference with Miriam, Aaron, and Moses? Who seems to have been the leader of the plot to weaken Moses' authority? How did God punish Miriam? How did he also show mercy?

**5.** Miriam seemed to demand too much recognition for her leadership role. How much praise do you expect for your contributions to your home, your church, and your job? How do you balance the need to encourage one another in good works with the command to glorify God alone in everything we do?

**6.** After the account of Miriam's restoration to the camp of the Israelites, she is not mentioned again until her death in Numbers 20. Do you think she continued to prophesy? Justify your answer.

**7.** What is your attitude toward your church leaders? Are you supportive with your cooperation or subversive of their positions with your criticism? What lessons from Miriam's life challenge you to develop a more effective partnership with other leaders to spread God's message?

A study of Moses' sister Miriam more aptly deserves the title, "Woman with Messages." Both as a young girl and as an old woman Miriam delivered messages, sometimes prompted by God and sometimes driven by her own ambition. How do we distinguish between God's direction and our own desires? How bold should we be in exercising our natural abilities and spiritual gifts? Miriam learned the hard way that God had richly endowed her with talent in order to accomplish his holy purposes and not her petty ones. Her example is both a stern warning and a great encouragement for us today.

## Identity Described

Miriam was Moses' elder sister. Though she is not named in Exodus 2, we assume it was she who stood at a distance to see what would happen to him after the baby Moses was placed in a papyrus basket among the reeds along the bank of the Nile. When Pharaoh's daughter discovered the baby, Miriam stepped forward and asked, "Shall I go and get one of the Hebrew women to nurse the baby for you?" Although it was her mother Jochebed who had engineered the scheme to save Moses and had carefully rehearsed Miriam in her role, the success of the rescue mission depended heavily on the girl's poise, charm, and articulate self-expression. She had to be in the right place at the right time, using the right words and manner to impress the princess. God delivered Israel's future deliverer through Miriam's perfect delivery of his message.

After Moses was weaned, his stepmother the princess brought him up in the palace. He received the best education Egyptian aristocracy could command (Acts 7:22). But he never forgot his Hebrew identity. When he was forty years old he killed an Egyptian in defense of a Hebrew slave and fled Egypt. For forty years he lived in exile in Midian, tending his father-in-law's sheep. His national and family ties were renewed only after God appeared in the burning bush and ordered Moses to return to Egypt to redeem Israel. It was Aaron the Levite, Moses' brother, whom God appointed to be spokesman to the people. Aaron was eighty-three years old and Moses was eighty by that time. Miriam is not mentioned as a participant in their reunion or commission.

Where was Miriam during those eighty years of Moses' separation from the family? She is identified in Exodus 15 as "Miriam the prophetess, Aaron's sister." This description allows us to speculate concerning Miriam's position among the Hebrews during much of that period. Of course, she was Moses' sister, too, but Aaron would have been considered the ranking male in the family before Moses returned from Midian, so her name was more closely linked to Aaron's. Being a prophetess, Miriam was one who spoke God's message to the people. The combination of these two attributes, sister to Aaron and a prophetess, indicates a position of prominence. She was both a natural and a spiritual leader.

During the Exodus from Egypt, after the crossing of the Red Sea, Moses celebrated the triumph with an exciting victory song. Miriam spontaneously grabbed a tambourine and led all the women around the camp in a joyful chorus, "Sing to the LORD, for he is highly exalted. The horse and its rider he has hurled into the sea . . ." (Ex. 15:21). Again, we are impressed with her charisma, which drew everyone to follow and rejoice with her. In this case, Miriam led her followers in support of Moses' leadership and in praise of God.

## Unity Disrupted

Unfortunately, this family unity and devotion were not always evident in Miriam's ministry. The power

138

and prestige of Moses' position impressed her, particularly when it appeared to overshadow hers. She and Aaron had been significant leaders among the Hebrews while they were in Egypt. Shouldn't the glories of leadership have continued to be shared equally within the family when the nation was finally on the move to freedom? After all, Aaron was a priest and Miriam a prophetess. With Moses in the role of general executive, a tripartite government of siblings was in view—prophetess, priest, and king. Miriam and Aaron were already experienced in their roles. In fact, the only reluctant member was Moses, who admitted to feelings of inadequacy for the task. So, to Miriam it made sense for Moses to share more of the responsibility and the glory with his brother and sister, especially since he had just delegated considerable authority to seventy judges to help him rule.

Miriam probably nursed her resentment for a long time, and searched for ways to assert her rights and utilize her gifts from the Lord to help his people. We, too, chafe when our good ideas and willingness to lead them to fruition are met with coolness by our fellow church members. But listen to God explain through Miriam's example how he intends to communicate his plan for the orderly administration of his work. He does not want us to use the talents he has given us for our selfish purposes rather than for his glory. Jealous ambition has no part in his kingdom.

Numbers 12:1 states, "Miriam and Aaron began to talk against Moses because of his Cushite wife." Miriam is named first in this case, suggesting that she was the instigator of the trouble. Actually, the root of the problem was not at all that the lady in question was a Cushite, nor even that she was Moses' wife. It is possible that her entry into the family somehow got in the way of Miriam's plans for power. It is more probable that Miriam and Aaron simply used her presence as a means of undermining Moses' position of respect in the eyes of the people in order to advance their own status. In political maneuvers, slander is an all-too-common tactic. When Miriam and Aaron spoke out publicly against Moses, they didn't even mention his wife. Their true motivation is exposed clearly by their words in Numbers 12:2: "Has the LORD spoken only through Moses? Hasn't he also spoken through us?" Thus they planted their poisonous seeds of discontent in soil already tainted with their own bitterness.

Women strong in the Lord sometimes question in their hearts whether the spiritual leaders in their homes or churches have disproportionately more authority than they, and wonder if their own gifts and rights deserve to be more widely recognized and uti-lized. If you have such feelings, take heed of this passage in Numbers 12. Open your hearts now to the Lord's teaching through Miriam and consider the consequences of her rebellion.

"Now the man Moses was very meek, above all the men which were upon the face of the earth" (Num. 12:3, KJV). This verse is no doubt familiar, but did you recall that it appears in this context? The meekest man on earth! Miriam and Aaron's challenge did not threaten him a bit. He was not on any ego trip. He had not campaigned for his office; in fact, he had tried to get out of his commission (see Ex. 3–4). God had persuaded him to serve by assuring him of his constant presence and power. It was never in Moses' mind to cut off his brother and sister from leadership. Years before, his anxiety about returning to Egypt had been eased only when God had promised that Aaron would be his spokesman to the people. Now Moses had delegated some of his authority to the seventy judges, and he would have welcomed the continued support of Miriam and Aaron, but only if their motives had been in line with God's plans. They were not.

"And the LORD heard this." My children have frequently asked me, "How do you always seem to know when we are up to some mischief?" My answer is twofold. "First, God always knows where you are and what you are doing, and sometimes he tells me so that I can care for you; second, I used to be a child myself." But better than mothers, our loving, omnipresent, omniscient Father sees and hears all we do outwardly, and he knows our inmost feelings. "Nothing in all creation is hidden from God's sight" (Heb. 4:13). Notice how amazed David was at God's intimate knowledge of him.

> O LORD, thou hast searched me, and known me.
> Thou knowest my downsitting and mine uprising,
> Thou understandest my thought afar off.
> Thou compassest my path and my lying down, and
>     art acquainted with all my ways.
> For there is not a word in my tongue, but, lo,
>     O LORD, thou knowest it altogether (Ps. 139:1–4,
>     KJV).

"And the LORD heard this." When we confide some juicy gossip to a friend, we may say, "This is just between you, me, and the lamppost." But the Lord hears every word. Or we may jest, "While the cat's away, the mice will play," thinking we may get away with changing the rules or lowering the standards when a person to whom we are responsible is out of town. But the Lord sees every act of mischief or deceit, a truth that should comfort us, for it is in keeping with God's concern for us at every moment.

"And the LORD heard this." Of course, he did not just *happen* to hear it, nor did he *have* to hear it. He already knew perfectly well the raging thoughts and feelings within the hearts of Miriam and Aaron before they spoke out. Why, then, did he wait until the crisis became so acute and divisive before dealing with it? Surely he could have nipped it in the bud with a timely, gentle warning before it erupted, or else have done away with the perpetrators before they could do much damage. Instead, God allowed the sore to fester until the fullness of time when its seriousness and ugliness would be most graphically demonstrated and dealt with to impress all Israel with its potential danger and the necessity of firm correction. Miriam, whose name means "obstinacy, rebellion," was allowed to experience the fullest consequences of her selfish ambition after it was manifest in its most extreme form. God's timing is perfect.

When God takes action, it is decisive. In response to Miriam's rebellious utterance, God called an emergency summit conference, ordering Miriam, Aaron, and Moses into his presence in the Tent of Meeting. Do you suppose that for a moment Miriam dared hope that she might win her case? But God said,

> When a prophet of the LORD is among you,
> I reveal myself to him in visions,
> I speak to him in dreams.
> But this is not true of my servant Moses;
> he is faithful in all my house,
> With him I speak face to face,
> clearly and not in riddles;
> he sees the form of the LORD.
> Why then were you not afraid to speak
> against my servant Moses? (Num. 12:6–8).

We are also told, "The anger of the LORD burned against them and he left them." How dreadful to kindle such anger in the Lord that he would depart! What greater punishment could he impose?

## Mercy Displayed

As we come face to face with God's wrath in this passage, let us also notice his great mercy. First he acknowledged Miriam's gifts as legitimate. She had been called a prophetess earlier, and so she was. Here God began by explaining how he reveals himself to prophets and prophetesses. He did not belittle her role or set aside her ministry. But Moses was a different matter entirely; with him God had a unique relationship that Miriam could not touch. It was not her challenge to Moses' authority that angered God so much as the rebellious attitude against God himself that her questions displayed. God was stating that it was Miriam's business to prophesy, but not her place

143

to thwart God's design for the leadership of his people by speaking against his special friend.

God's anger and his departure were terrible enough, but there was also a third reaction to Miriam's sin. "When the cloud lifted from above the Tent, there stood Miriam—leprous, like snow" (Num. 12:10). Again we notice that Aaron was spared this shame, a further indication that he was less guilty than his sister. Yet, he identified with her when he asked Moses to intercede for her, saying, "Please, my lord, do not hold against *us* the sin *we* have so foolishly committed" (Num. 12:11, italics added). God's mercy was demonstrated once more when Miriam was healed and restored after only seven days of isolation outside the camp of the Israelites. She must have endured enormous pain and disgrace, but she was not utterly abandoned. Numbers 12:15 adds: "And the people did not move on till she was brought back."

## Utility Diminished

Forty years elapse before the Bible mentions Miriam again, and then it is only to record her death in Numbers 20. In that chapter Moses himself disobeyed God by striking the rock at Meribah, which caused him to be barred from entry into Canaan. His pride was showing when he cried to the people, "Listen, you rebels, must *we* bring you water out of this rock?" (Num. 20:10, italics added). God rebuked him severely.

Because you did not trust in me enough to honor me as
holy in the sight of the Israelites, you will not bring this
community into the land I give them (Num. 20:12).

Clearly, Miriam was not the only person to err in
exaggerated self-importance or to doubt God's power
and purpose. Over and over again the Bible shows us
the inevitable result of such lack of faith. God endows
men and women with natural abilities and spiritual
gifts to accomplish his will. Each individual has the
choice either to devote his or her talents to God's service or to seek his or her own glory.

The eyes of the LORD range throughout the earth to
strengthen those whose hearts are fully committed to
him (2 Chron. 16:9).

But he will withdraw his support from those who mis-
judge or misapply his gifts.

Miriam was restored to the camp, and she and the
Israelites wandered the wilderness for forty years. But
there is no further mention of her prophesying. Perhaps God removed this gift from her, as indicated by
Christ's teaching:

With the measure you use, it will be measured to
you—and even more. Whoever has will be given
more; whoever does not have, even what he has will be
taken from him (Mark 4:24–25).

Or perhaps Miriam sulked, refusing to make use of her
ability to prophesy, unwilling to accept God's total
cleansing and acceptance after her humiliation. The

silence at the end of her story makes us wonder whether the reconciliation of her heart to God was as complete as her physical restoration to the Israelite camp. We, too, should consider how we respond to God's offer of forgiveness following a rebuke, and whether we return to wholehearted commitment or withdraw from service.

Miriam died without adding a chorus to Moses' final song in Deuteronomy 32. She never entered the Promised Land. But Micah 6:4 reminds us of her former greatness, ranking her with her brothers in the vanguard of the Exodus. "I brought you up out of Egypt and redeemed you from the land of slavery. I sent Moses to lead you, also Aaron and Miriam." We should be greatly encouraged by Miriam's example of boldness in delivering God's messages and in singing his praises. At the same time, we must beware of the temptation to speak forth out of our own minds and ambitions, rather than through his inspiration, lest our ministry be cut short because of our selfishness.

Miriam was indeed a woman with messages. As a small child, as an old woman, and as a prophetess, she spoke boldly and persuasively. Her intelligence, insight, and charisma are apparent at every point. The problem was that sometimes (Num. 12) her jealousy overruled her better judgment. Self-centeredness preempted submission. She was rebuked by God and set aside from his service when she was carried away by her self-importance instead of being ruled by her message from God. Now she has a message for us. What encouragement and warning do you receive from the story of her life? How has God endowed you with his spiritual and physical gifts, and for what special area of work for him? Are they dedicated to his glory?

# 11

## Abigail

### Primary Scripture Reading

1 Samuel 25

### Supplementary References

Judges 14
2 Samuel 20
Luke 1:38; 6:27–36

### Questions for Study and Discussion

**1.** Describe Nabal and Abigail as a husband-and-wife team. How did Nabal antagonize David? What did Abigail do? Do you agree with the decisions she made both before and after she went to David the first time? How could a wife be both righteous before the Lord and respectful of her unbelieving husband?

**2.** How did Abigail approach David? Was she more concerned for him or for herself? How does this scene illustrate Christ's instruction to love your enemy? What happened as a result of this approach?

**3.** How was Abigail's haste an important factor in the success of the mission? What did David think of her quickness

(1 Sam. 25:34)? Sometimes "haste makes waste." Sometimes she "who hesitates is lost." Is your normal response to a critical situation impulsive, deliberate, careless, lethargic, vigorous, evasive? Knowing that your reaction impresses people around you, how should you adjust your behavior?

**4.** Notice that Abigail called herself David's handmaid— (KJV; maidservant—NIV). Do you know of another woman who used that term to describe herself in the Bible? Are you a handmaid to anyone? How do you feel about the term and the role? To whom are you willing to bow in humility and service?

**5.** How was Abigail able to influence David to reverse his decision to attack? Compare her actions to the approaches taken by women in 2 Samuel 20:16–22 and Judges 14:16–17 to change a man's mind. Why and how do you try to influence key people in your life?

**6.** How did God use Abigail to recall David to a better sense of his purpose? Compare what Abigail said about the Lord with her description of David as "my lord" in 1 Samuel 25.

**7.** How was Abigail rewarded for her motives, her methods, and her message? What rewards have you received for speaking God's message with appropriate boldness and humility?

Powerful public ministries such as Deborah's or Miriam's are not part of God's design for every man and woman. Yet, each one of us is called upon to reflect and relay his message in whatever place he may put us. The biblical example of Abigail teaches us that we must be prepared for and sensitive to emergencies in order to communicate effectively when decisive moments arrive. Abigail's timely, tactful appeal to David rescued her household from destruction and reversed

David's course from revenge to rejoicing. Her story encourages us to evaluate the timing and tone of our own message-ministry.

Abigail's story is recorded in 1 Samuel 25. During a period of relief from King Saul's pursuit of him, David and his followers protected shepherds belonging to a man named Nabal. When shearing season arrived, David approached Nabal expecting an invitation to share in the festivities. Nabal rudely refused David and his people any hospitality in return. Outraged at such an insult, David ordered his men to put on swords and cut down all the men of Nabal's household. Abigail, Nabal's wife, was informed of the crisis by the servants, who also indicated the justice of David's claim. She acted quickly and arrived at David's camp just in time to placate him with her words and gifts of food. David decided not to carry out his attack, but instead praised God and sent Abigail home in peace. When Nabal heard what had happened, he suffered an apparent heart attack from the shock. He died ten days later, and Abigail became David's wife.

What are the key qualities of Abigail's character and message that combined to make her such an effective agent of change? We shall consider her traits of hope, haste, humility, and honor.

## Hope

If you were suddenly informed that four hundred armed warriors were about to murder your husband and all the male servants of your large estate, and probably kidnap you and all the women and children, how would you respond? Panic? Despair? Recognizing that, according to the customs of the day, Nabal fully deserved the punishment he was about to receive, why didn't Abigail just give up and simply throw herself at David's feet, begging only that her own life be spared?

Thinking further along these lines, might Abigail have felt a twinge of relief as she contemplated the possibility of surviving her personal ordeal of oppression under Nabal's roof? No other biblical couple appears to have been as mismatched as this wife and husband. Consider Nabal's character, described in Samuel 25 (KJV): "A man in Maon, whose possessions were in Carmel; and the man was very great;" "churlish and evil in his doings;" "evil is determined against our master, and against all his household: for he is such a son of Belial, that a man cannot speak to him;" "this man of Belial,[1] even Nabal: for as his name is, so is he; Nabal is his name, and folly is with him" ("nabal" means "fool, dolt"). In short, Nabal was wealthy and wicked.

What a contrast to Abigail, who is described as "a woman of good understanding, and of a beautiful countenance." Nabal was obstinate and offensive, but Abigail was sensitive and approachable, willing to listen and respond to the needs of her household. Realizing that Nabal had created a crisis, she reacted with action rather than apathy, revealing her inner attitude of hope in God, in David's character, and in her own ability to make a difference. Instead of feeling helpless

---

1. Unger says this phrase indicates a worthless, lawless fellow.

in your adverse circumstances, can you follow Abigail's example and evaluate the hopeful aspects of your situation, concentrating your energies on the things that *can* be changed?

## Haste

Abigail's mission was successful because her response was immediate. The servants reported to her Nabal's rudeness and David's resolve to have vengeance.

> Then Abigail made haste, and took two hundred loaves, and two bottles of wine, and five sheep ready dressed, and five measures of parched corn, and an hundred clusters of raisins, and two hundred cakes of figs, and laid them on asses (1 Sam. 25:18, KJV).

Two points regarding her haste are significant. First, Abigail was prepared. Unlike Mother Hubbard in the nursery rhyme, who had nothing to offer her poor dog, Abigail had obviously managed her domestic duties so well that her cupboards were full. Notice that everything she brought to David required considerable time and care to prepare. The loaves must have already been baked, the wine aged, the sheep dressed, the grain roasted, the raisins dried, and the fig cakes pressed. There could be no question of a quick stop at the corner delicatessen or a feeble apology to the effect that she meant well but had nothing to offer. Abigail was able to provide a delicious home-made banquet instantaneously for David and his men because it was all ready ahead of time, and thereby proved the sincerity of her words and her heart. Her habit of preparedness combined effectively with her haste to appease the hunger as well as the anger of her future king.

The second aspect of Abigail's haste is her proper sense of priorities. She perceived the urgency of the servants' appeal and stopped what she was doing to respond with her full attention and energy. Sometimes we exercise our hope in God while we wait patiently for his provision; sometimes he expects us to exercise our faith actively by hurrying to do his will. The Holy Spirit enables us to discern which response is appropriate.

Besides admiring Abigail for her preparation and the priorities that allowed her to hurry, we should recognize that her haste was a crucial ingredient to her success. It was necessary as well as admirable. There was no time to lose and Abigail lost none. David appreciated the importance of her quick action.

> For in very deed, as the LORD God of Israel liveth, which hath kept me back from hurting thee, *except thou hadst hasted* and come to meet me, surely there had not been left unto Nabal by the morning light any (man) (1 Sam. 25:34, KJV, italics added).

Finally, we see Abigail's habit of haste bearing fruit in a different sense. Instead of hurrying to avert disaster, she hurried to meet her master. After the death of Nabal, David sent word to Abigail that he desired to take her for his wife. Her verbal and physical responses are recorded in 1 Samuel 25:41–42.

> And she arose, and bowed herself on her face to the earth, and said, Behold, let thine handmaid be a servant to wash the feet of the servants of my lord. *And Abigail hasted,* and arose, and rode upon an ass, with five damsels of hers that went after her; and she went after the messengers of David and became his wife (KJV, italics added).

What a compliment we pay those whom we love or respect when we respond to them and their needs quickly!

## Humility

In response to David's proposal of marriage Abigail referred to herself as his handmaid. Her willingness to submit and serve him are apparent from her very first approach to David.

> And when Abigail saw David, she hasted, and lighted off the ass, and fell before David on her face, and bowed herself to the ground and fell at his feet, and said, Upon me, my lord, upon me let this iniquity be: and let thine handmaid, I pray thee, speak in thine audience, and hear the words of thine handmaid (1 Sam. 25:23–24, KJV).

Physically, Abigail humbled herself before David by bowing to the ground at his feet. Six times in her appeal she called herself David's handmaid. Of course, this phrase was appropriate to her time and circumstances. More beautiful to note is her attitude of humility, demonstrated in her request that Nabal's offense be counted as her own. She was willing to place herself at David's mercy for her husband's sake as well as for her own, even though she must have considered that her chances for survival would surely have been enhanced had she separated her cause from Nabal's.

In the New Testament, Mary responded to the angel's announcement of Jesus' birth with the words, "Behold, the handmaid of the Lord; be it unto me according to thy word" (Luke 1:38, KJV). Unfortunately, many women today resist the implication of the term *handmaid*. Abigail's acceptance of this position of dependence was not based solely on the desperateness of her situation. It was not demeaning for her to be truly humble, even though it is clear that she was a highly talented and independent woman. Let us examine our own hearts for pride that might prevent us from being effective deliverers of God's message through our words and the ways we live our lives. We may ask if we are willful instead of willing, limiting our effectiveness for God's service by our refusal to be humble before him and others.

### Honor

Abigail's behavior honored God, David, and her husband. The King James Version uses the term *lord* fourteen times and LORD seven times in her moving speech to David. Even more striking than the numbers is the attributes she assigned to each one. Notice what she said about David:

Unto me, my *lord*, let this iniquity be . . .

let not my *lord* . . . regard this man . . .

I . . . saw not the young men of my *lord*, whom thou
didst send . . .

Now therefore, my *lord*, . . . let thine enemies, and
they that seek evil to my *lord*, be as Nabal.

. . . this blessing . . . brought my *lord*, let it even be
given unto the young men that follow my *lord*.

. . . the LORD will certainly make my *lord* a sure house;
because my *lord* fighteth the battles of the LORD, and
evil hath not been found in thee all thy days.

. . . the soul of my *lord* shall be bound in the bundle of
life. . . .

. . . when the LORD shall have done to my *lord* according to all the good that he hath spoken . . . and shall
have appointed thee ruler over Israel;

That this shall be no grief . . . nor offense of heart unto
my *lord* . . .

or that my *lord* hath avenged himself:

but when the LORD shall have dealt well with my *lord*
. . . remember . . . (1 Sam. 25:24–31, KJV, italics
added).

Would you think of praising your potential enemy
so respectfully and meaning it so sincerely? Abigail

complimented David both for his former reputation and for his future position. She expressed confidence that his righteous character would prevent him from committing an act that he would later regret. Abigail was not merely employing a shrewd stratagem to pacify an unstable outlaw; she was sensitively encouraging this offended man by recalling him to a better sense of his own nature and purpose. She did this by reminding him of God's nature and purpose. Notice these descriptions:

as the LORD liveth . . .

seeing the LORD hath withholden thee from coming to shed blood, and from avenging thyself with thine own hand . . .

the LORD will certainly make my lord a sure house; because my lord fighteth the battles of the LORD . . .

the soul of my lord shall be bound in the bundle of life with the LORD thy God . . .

when the LORD shall have done to my lord according to all the good that he hath spoken concerning thee, and shall have appointed thee ruler over Israel . . .

when the LORD shall have dealt well with my lord . . . (1 Sam. 25:26–31, KJV).

Abigail gave glory to God as the living Lord who protects, provides, preserves, promises, and promotes. She made subtle reference to David's prior experiences battling Goliath and running from Saul. (See 1 Sam. 16–19, 24 for these stories.) David was uplifted by Abigail's positive words, which so reverently connected him with his God.

But can we say that Abigail honored her husband also? Did she not act without his permission, almost repudiating his authority over his household and his right to withhold hospitality? What kind of wife would hasten to serve a banquet to the men her husband had so rudely rejected? To behave so independently, even secretly, is surely an indication of disregard, which must be the opposite of honor, is it not? And if we still hesitate to rebuke her, what can we say about her calling Nabal a fool? To call one's husband that term in front of his enemies could hardly be considered respectful. Doesn't Abigail's own mouth condemn her?

Admittedly, it is hard to argue against such evidence, but it may be worth our time to consider a broader perspective, which takes into account the extremity of the crisis. Abigail could not deny Nabal's nasty character. His rudeness was inexcusable and was just cause for revenge according to the social customs of that day. Abigail's honesty in acknowledging this point was an effective opening statement for her appeal. Clearly, she knew her mate and measured carefully whether and when to inform him of her actions. Had she consulted her husband about reconsidering his position or authorizing her mission, there is little doubt that he would have angrily refused. Their doom loomed large from the next hill, for David had commanded his men to destroy Nabal's people. Abigail demonstrated her loyalty to her husband, not through unity with him but through identification with him, when she begged David to consider Nabal's offense as being upon her own head. Perhaps Abigail did fail to treat Nabal with full respect, but she did at least try to save his life.

A second point in her defense is that Abigail returned to Nabal after her visit with David. She waited for the best time to inform him of the success of her mission—when he was sober. Even so, his heart "died within him" at the news. Abigail undoubtedly helped nurse Nabal during the ten days before his death. Allowing God to oversee the fulfillment of his promises, Abigail remained faithful to her husband until God removed him.

## Hearkening

What was the outcome of Abigail's hope, haste, humility, and honor? The Bible gives us a beautiful conclusion to the interview.

And David said to Abigail, Blessed be the LORD God of Israel, which sent thee this day to meet me: And blessed be thy advice, and blessed be thou, which hast kept me this day from coming to shed blood, and from avenging myself with mine own hand. . . . So David received of her hand that which she had brought him, and said unto her, Go up in peace to thine house; see, *I have hearkened to thy voice,* and have accepted thy person (1 Sam. 25:32–35, KJV, italics added).

What better result can we hope for in our Christian lives, than that our God, our advice, and our persons will be blessed, and that those we contact will accept and apply to their lives our words and our living examples? What further satisfaction we should experience if we were to be such agents of peace!

# 12

## Naaman's Maid

### Primary Scripture Reading

2 Kings 5

### Supplementary References

Matthew 18:1–5
Luke 4:24–27; 9:46–48

### Questions for Study and Discussion

**1.** Who was Naaman, and what was his problem?

**2.** What can you discover about Naaman's maid? What did she know about the God of Israel? What did she tell Naaman to do?

**3.** What risks did Naaman's maid face in presenting her message? How was she protected? What have you risked to tell someone about God's saving power?

**4.** How did the message become distorted in transmission from the maid to her mistress and master, then to the kings of Syria and Israel? How did it get straightened out? How has God's truth overcome obstacles for you?

**5.** List the sequence of steps in Naaman's actual cure. What nearly caused Naaman to miss it? What was the turning point of his life?

**6.** Do you think the relationship of Naaman to his maid was any different after his return? How might she have reacted to his cure? Have you ever played a part in God's miracle of physical or spiritual healing?

**7.** How can rank affect a person's ability to be an effective agent of God's message? Consider Naaman's maid in the light of Matthew 18:1–5 and Luke 9:46–48. How does her story encourage and challenge you?

A single verse of Scripture offers a tiny glimpse rather than a full biographical sketch. Without making too much of Naaman's young maid, we can discover in her story several important principles concerning how God's messages are transmitted through his servants. Naaman's servant girl was not a major protagonist in II Kings 5, but she did initiate a complex chain of events that culminated in her master's triumphant affirmation of faith.

## Truth Bears Fruit

A seed consists of an embryo that contains the reproducible life substance of the plant, to be nourished by the endosperm and protected by an outer covering. This tough skin or shell can take quite a beating without allowing any harm to the embryo inside, so that even after going through an extended period of hardship—such as being in adverse weather, rocky soil, or inadequate moisture—the seed can still germinate when conditions improve. At the beginning of 2 Kings 5 we see the kernel of God's truth, contained within the heart of Naaman's servant girl, still safe after a series of unfavorable circumstances.

> Now Naaman was commander of the army of the king of Aram. He was a great man in the sight of his master and highly regarded, because through him the LORD had given victory to Aram. He was a valiant soldier, but he had leprosy. Now bands from Aram had gone out and had taken captive a young girl from Israel, and she served Naaman's wife (2 Kings 5:1–2).

Note the many obstacles working against this girl's ministry. First, she was an Israelite captive in Syria, the enemy of her people. She was a slave. She was a girl. And she was young. What chance did her message have when it came from someone of the wrong age, sex, rank, religion, and national origin? She risked being ignored, teased, or punished for daring to speak up at all. Yet the truth *persevered* and was heard.

The second obstacle was the limitation of her knowledge of God. To her mistress she said, "If only my master would see the prophet who is in Samaria! He would cure him of his leprosy." But this was not the whole story, not then nor today. God may work through prophets or doctors, through men or medicine, but the power to heal and restore is his alone. The servant girl may have spoken more from partial ignorance or in deference to Elisha's reputation than from her own experience of faith, but she spoke with full assurance, and the truth *penetrated* the darkness to offer the hope that sent Naaman on his way to Israel.

The third obstacle was the number of stages in the transmission of the young girl's message. She spoke with Naaman's wife, who told her husband, who talked to the king of Syria, who sent Naaman with a letter to his enemy the king of Israel. By that time the message read, "With this letter I am sending my servant Naaman to you so that you may cure him of his leprosy." Obviously, something had been lost in translation, as now neither God *nor* his prophet was mentioned, but the king himself was presumed—possibly mockingly—to possess curative powers. No wonder the king panicked! As in the children's game Telephone, some static (here in the form of spiritual deafness or disbelief) distorted or interrupted the connection at one of the "switchboards." The king of Israel, instead of redirecting Naaman in his search for God's healing, tore his robes in desperation and cried out,

> Am I God? Can I kill and bring back to life? Why does this fellow send someone to me to be cured of his leprosy? See how he is trying to pick a quarrel with me! (2 Kings 5:7).

A beginning student of electricity learns that current flows only when three things are present: a power source, a load to use the power (lightbulb, motor, etc.), and a conductor, all forming a continuous circuit. Power is cut off from the load when there is a break in the line. When the king of Israel broke the circuit of

God's power in Naaman's life, indicating his own lack of insight and faith, God worked through Elisha from the terminal on the other end to reconnect the wires.

> When Elisha the man of God heard that the king of Israel had torn his robes, he sent him this message: "Why have you torn your robes? Have the man come to me and he will know that there is a prophet in Israel" (2 Kings 5:8).

Thus, the transmission of God's power was successfully completed. The life in the seed of truth planted by Naaman's servant girl was *preserved*.

In the same way, when we speak with assurance of that which we know about God, the smallest expression of our faith may become the impetus through which another person discovers the way, the truth, and the life. God's miraculous, life-giving truth can overcome such obstacles as adverse circumstances, ignorance, and interference to persevere, penetrate, and preserve its saving power, for ourselves and for others.

## Truth Takes Root

Naaman went to a lot of trouble to get through to God's prophet, and he was furious at Elisha's refusal to see him, not to mention his failure to work magic over him. Naaman's pride in his position and in his own perseverance on this occasion nearly prevented him from accepting God's gift of healing when it required of him no effort or price. Because he at first refused to humble himself by entering the Jordan River, he al-

167

most failed the prophet's test of humility which must precede faith to bring about a cure.

Many believers have seen in Naaman's story a picture of how a Christian can accept Christ's free gift of cleansing and salvation only in a spirit of true submission. God had protected the little seed of his truth, which the servant girl planted, through many unfavorable circumstances. Finally, the conditions began to change. Naaman's heart opened in obedience and he accepted the prophet's prescription to wash himself seven times in the Jordan River (at the urging of his servants, we note again). He was physically restored, spiritually healed. As the water symbolically reached down into the seed of truth in his heart, new life and faith burst forth for Naaman. His cognitive response of faith was as miraculous as the healing itself. Both were the result of God's grace when he said, "Now I *know* that there is no God in all the world except in Israel" (2 Kings 5:15, italics added). Having humbled himself by simple obedience, he went on to real faith in God and so gained access to the presence of God's prophet at last.

Do we share Naaman's conviction? Francis Schaeffer has said that only the empty hands of faith can receive the full measure of God's grace. We must learn to release our hold on our possessions and our positions, and accept his gift of eternal life. Psalm 116:12-13 (KJV) says, "What shall I render unto the LORD for all of his benefits toward me? I will take the cup of salvation, and call upon the name of the LORD."

What else does a seed require in order to grow, besides water and sunshine? Soil, of course, and that is the next thing Naaman desired.

Please let me, your servant, be given as much *earth* as a pair of mules can carry, for your servant will never again make burnt offerings and sacrifices to any other god but the LORD (2 Kings 5:17, italics added).

Naaman still had much to learn *about* the Lord, but his faith *in* him was securely planted. Undoubtedly, the little servant girl could see the fruit borne of her simple message in her master's changed life, which would in turn nourish her own faith. This cross-pollination of blessings can be a reality in our lives, too, as we grow through sharing with others God's truth, grace, and peace.

# 13

## Naomi

### Primary Scripture Reading

Ruth 1–4

### Supplementary References

Luke 22:31–32
2 Corinthians 12:1–10
Hebrews 12:1–12

### Questions for Study and Discussion

**1.** Why did Naomi go to Moab? What series of events made her decide to return to Bethlehem? What emotions might she have had that influenced her decision?

**2.** Describe Naomi's relationships with her two daughters-in-law. Why did she urge them both to return to their homes, but later accept Ruth's plea to remain with her? How would you differentiate urging from nagging?

**3.** List the attributes of God that are either stated explicitly or implied in the Book of Ruth. How did Naomi testify to God's grace during both her good times and bad? What is your experience with God, and how is your life a witness to others?

**4.** Was it true that the LORD's hand had gone out against Naomi? How did he also bless her? How do you reconcile God's power with the presence of evil in the world? Why does he allow his people to suffer?

**5.** What influence did Naomi have on Ruth? What influence did Ruth have on Naomi? How have you been blessed with a similar friendship?

**6.** Who was Boaz? List the sequence of events by which he became the kinsman-redeemer. Did Naomi and Ruth act appropriately or inconsistently with God's plan concerning Boaz?

**7.** Of all the women in this study, which one has meant the most to you, either as a comfort or a challenge? Why? How have these studies encouraged you by providing a personal application of the Bible to your life? In what ways have you drawn closer to God through them?

Some Christians may imagine that we should only speak for the Lord when we are experiencing success in our lives, and that it would be better to remain silent when we are struggling or suffering lest we give God a bad name. We worry that our faith is valuable to others only when it demonstrates our personal victory, and forget that it is Christ's sure and final victory that should always be our focus.

Naomi was not a prophetess, yet her life has a message that is both profound and practical for our day. She experienced extensive personal hardship and endured periods of depression, yet she continued to praise and trust God for his blessings wherever she found them. She was honest in expressing her true feelings, which were not always pleasant, but she never lost all hope. She was sensitive, sincere, un-selfish—an ideal mother-in-law. Her witness was winsome; Ruth, her daughter-in-law, was drawn by her beautiful character to share first faith with Naomi, and then her future and her family.

## Faith

The Book of Ruth, in which Naomi's story is found, opens with a famine in Judah, during the days when the judges ruled. The nation of Moab had already caused repeated difficulties for Israel (Num. 21–25, Judg. 3). God had warned his people not to have any dealings with the Moabites, and not to marry foreign wives. Nevertheless, when the famine became severe, a man named Elimelech decided to take his wife Naomi and his two sons to Moab, expecting that he could better provide for them there. But he died, and his sons married Moabite women, Orpah and Ruth. About ten years later the sons also died, "and Naomi was left without her two sons and her husband" (Ruth 1:5).

The opening verses of the Book of Ruth suggest that Naomi was not a woman to stir up controversy in her family. She would probably have obeyed quietly when her husband announced the move to Moab, and after his death remained quietly in the home of her sons and their pagan wives. She was not the type to preach at them concerning their disregard of God's directions, nor would she have tried to usurp their authority over their households. If the men had survived, Naomi probably would not have spoken up at all. But while she was quiet, and later when she was alone, she kept her ears and her heart open for news of God's work.

> When she heard in Moab that the LORD had come to the aid of his people by providing food for them, Naomi and her daughters-in-law prepared to return home from there (Ruth 1:6).

Thus, two events put Naomi back on the road to her home in Bethlehem: the deaths of her husband and sons, and the report of God's provision for his people in Judah. There was nothing to keep her in Moab any longer, and every reason for her to return to Judah.

For Orpah and Ruth the decision was much more difficult. They had spent more than ten years with Naomi, and they undoubtedly felt very close to her as well as obligated to continue caring for their mother-in-law. However, their own family and national ties were in Moab; they would not have been eager to live as widows and foreigners in Judah, no matter how much they loved Naomi. Naomi's gentle sensitivity to these mixed emotions was manifest when she allowed Orpah and Ruth to start out on the journey with her.

> Then Naomi said to her two daughters-in-law, "Go back, each of you, to your mother's house. May the LORD show kindness to you, as you have shown to your dead and to me. May the LORD grant that each of you will find rest in the home of another husband" (Ruth 1:8–9).

The younger women wept aloud and insisted on going with her, but Naomi overruled them once again.

But Naomi said, "Return home, my daughters. Why would you come with me? Am I going to have any more sons, who could become your husbands? Return home, my daughters; I am too old to have another husband. Even if I thought there was still hope for me—even if I had a husband tonight and then gave birth to sons—would you wait until they grew up? No, my daughters. It is more bitter for me than for you, because the LORD's hand has gone out against me" (Ruth 1:11–13).

This time the two daughters-in-law responded differently from each other according to their contrasting temperaments. At first both women were prepared to go with Naomi out of a sense of duty and affection, but at Naomi's urging, Orpah turned back. We presume she remained in Moab with her own family, and perhaps married again, as Naomi had prayed she would. The Bible tells us nothing more about her. But Ruth persisted. Consider what must have been the tremendous impact of Naomi's life on Ruth during their years together, which moved Ruth to respond with these beautiful words:

"Don't urge me to leave you or to turn back from you. Where go I will go, and where you stay I will stay. Your people will be my people and your God my God. Where you die I will die, and there I will be buried. May the LORD deal with me, be it ever so severely, if anything but death separates you and me" (Ruth 1:16–17).

Naomi knew when to urge and when to stop urging. Three times she tried to persuade the women to stay in Moab. Orpah accepted the offer because it was reasonable, sensitive, and sincere. But Ruth was different. She said, "Don't urge me to leave." Naomi's sensitivity is shown once again in verse 18: "When Naomi realized that Ruth was determined to go with her, she stopped urging her." Instead of selfishly pushing her own preferences onto her daughters-in-law, Naomi watched and listened for signs of their true inclinations.

Naomi was not trying to outmaneuver or overpower her daughters-in-law. She simply allowed God to work through her life to touch them. Orpah and Ruth each had the same opportunity to become acquainted with God through Naomi's deep faith displayed in her day-to-day existence. But the seed fell on different kinds of soil (see Matt. 13). Orpah returned to her people and her gods; Ruth said, "Your people will be my people and your God my God."

If we sincerely ask God to use our lives to bear eternal fruit for him in the lives of others, we, too, must recognize the fact that some people will respond with open hearts while others will refuse the good news we want to share. We must be available, but also accepting of the time, methods, or people he chooses to relay his message (see 1 Cor. 3:5–9). Naomi could have become discouraged over her 50 percent failure in bringing her daughters-in-law to the Lord. Instead, she accepted each of their decisions without judgment or remorse.

When Naomi arrived in Bethlehem with Ruth, her former friends barely recognized her. "Can this be Naomi?" they wondered. Once again, Naomi's testimony was hardly triumphant, but it did express her deep awareness of God's activity in her life during her long absence from home.

> "Don't call me Naomi," she told them. "Call me Mara, because the Almighty has made my life very bitter. I went away full, but the LORD has brought me back empty. Why call me Naomi? The LORD has afflicted me; the Almighty has brought misfortune upon me" (Ruth 1:20–21).

What kind of winsome witness was this? It was honest. Through her trials in Moab—the deaths of her husband and sons, as well as their struggles to find food in a foreign land—Naomi had come to feel that the LORD's hand had gone out against her, which she had told Orpah and Ruth and repeated to her friends in Bethlehem. But she still felt that it was God's hand at work. There was real bitterness, to the point that Naomi requested that she be called Mara, which means "bitter," instead of her own name, which means "pleasant."

But Naomi never denied God's existence nor rejected the possibility of his blessing for others or herself at a later time. She saw no contradiction in her belief that God, who sometimes afflicted was also the one who provided and blessed. This truth had been verified by her experiences. Because Naomi was honest in sharing her sufferings, her friends were able to share all the more in her ultimate success, which we shall see at the end of her story.

## Fantasy

Think for a moment about Naomi's statement that God's hand had gone out against her. Was this mere fantasy, proof that her temporary depression was becoming paranoia? Can God's hand ever go against one of his people, or is it only Satan who brings misfortune and evil into the world? Do we not have one adversary and one advocate? How can our friend become our enemy?

The Bible has a great deal to teach on these crucial questions, more than we can explore in depth here. But we know that God is omnipotent, and that the domain of his power is not limited to working only in behalf of those who honor him. He has "set his hand," "kindled his anger," and "raised up enemies" against hundreds of individuals and nations who have rebelled against him, whether or not they were numbered among his chosen people. For example, see 1 Samuel 7:13 and Isaiah 5:25.

God sometimes does allow bad things to happen to his people today also, not for his own pleasure nor for our punishment, but always in perfect harmony with his character and purposes. We may feel the impact of these blows as a result of our deliberate choice to disregard or disobey God's authority over our lives, or we may simply become wounded in the crossfire as the battle rages around us in the world. None of us is immune. God knows that Satan desires to sift us like wheat (Luke 22:31–32) and he may give him limited permission to do so, as he did with Job, in order to bring us back into full commitment and service to himself. Romans 8:28 does not mean that our walk with God will necessarily always be in the sunshine.

Naomi was not accusing God of being mean to her; she was acknowledging that he was in control of her life and that she had suffered. This challenges us to honestly and realistically acknowledge the status of our walk with God, no matter how he may be dealing with us at the moment. Doing so is a more powerful testimony to his presence than any evangelistic formula we can recite. To have deep doubts and serious needs does not mean that our faith is weak. But faith does then become visible to ourselves as well as to others; for when we are most vulnerable we are also most transparent, and the often-painful process of God's tender dealing with his children is most readily observed. We must be willing to become small and to hurt in order to grow and be healed. Naomi's apparent weakness did not weaken her witness.

The connection between our pain and our praise does not mean that God wants us to rejoice over our sufferings *per se,* any more than we should rejoice over the sufferings of other people, which would be dishonest and cruel. But he does want us to rejoice in *him.* Always (Phil. 4:4–7). Amazingly, we find that we can endure any agony when we know God is with us in it, supplying his strength and love even when we do not comprehend his plan.

Naomi's attitude was both honest and contagious, and Ruth caught it. She was determined to share Naomi's life and faith, as indeed she already had. Her vow, "May the LORD deal with me, be it ever so severely, if anything but death separates you and me," was proof of her conversion. Naomi had not promised Ruth a life of ease, nor had she lived one. Ruth must have watched Naomi suffer and must have drawn on her strength through the years they had already shared. Naomi's sustaining faith in God had obviously impressed Ruth and brought her into fellowship with her Lord.

Throughout the Book of Ruth God's name is upheld as a source of life and blessing. Of the eighty-four verses in the book, sixteen speak of the Lord, either in affirmation or supplication. They tell that he provided food, showed kindness, gave offspring, enabled Ruth to conceive, and provided Naomi with a kinsman-redeemer; that he was asked to show kindness, to grant rest with new homes and husbands for Orpah and Ruth, to be with and to bless Boaz and his field workers, and to repay and reward Ruth for her kindness to Naomi; and that Ruth and Boaz each made a vow in the name of the Lord. Naomi's faith in an active, present, real, personal God permeates the story of Ruth and reaches out to our hearts as well. Can we say that others have "come to take refuge" under the wings of the Lord because of the honest, vibrant messages of our lives?

### Future and Family

When Ruth linked herself to Naomi by faith, she made a commitment to share the future with her, whatever happened. From that time on they functioned as a harmonious team. Chapter 2 of Ruth explains how their partnership developed. Ruth offered to glean, and Naomi approved. Ruth was successful working in Boaz' fields, and shared with Naomi not only the grain she had gathered but also the leftovers from the lunch Boaz had given her. Naomi was ready with words of praise to God for his providence and with encouragement and advice for Ruth. The two women lived in this way for some time, with Ruth working in the fields and Naomi managing their home. They seemed content; Naomi's outbursts of bitterness disappeared as she began to rest in God's care and Ruth's companionship.

From the start, when Naomi had set out for Bethlehem from Moab, she had made it clear to her daughters-in-law that the chances of providing husbands for them from her own family were nil. Nevertheless, Ruth insisted on remaining with Naomi, her people, and her God until death, without mentioning any desire for a husband or children of her own. When Naomi and Ruth settled down in Bethlehem, both of them expected to remain single.

But Naomi was still open to receive news of God's work. Just as she had once heard that he had come to the aid of his people in providing food, she began to realize that he might be coming to her aid once again in providing a kinsman-redeemer for her family. When she heard how kind Boaz had been to Ruth, a foreigner, in inquiring about her, protecting her, and making her task easier, as well as providing her lunch, Naomi praised God not only for his kindness but also for his kinship.

"The LORD bless him!" Naomi said to her daughter-in-law. "The LORD has not stopped his kindness to the living and the dead." She added, "That man is our close relative; he is one of our kinsman-redeemers" (Ruth 2:20).

Neither Ruth nor Naomi was a schemer who selfishly plotted to trap Boaz into marriage. But they were available to cooperate with God. The fact that Ruth "just happened" to work in Boaz's fields and to find favor in his eyes encouraged Naomi to suggest that God might have a greater purpose in mind. Similarly, when we trust in God, our eyes are opened to recognize his design in events that may appear to others to be mere coincidence.

Naomi gave Ruth careful instructions in how to approach Boaz at night on the threshing floor, which she obeyed perfectly. Boaz, too, was sensitive to God's leading, and as Naomi had predicted to Ruth, he did not let the matter rest until it was settled. The role of kinsman-redeemer included the right to redeem (buy) the land of a deceased relative, with the condition that offspring would be raised in his name so that no branch of a family would be cut off from property and heritage. Boaz offered the right of redeeming Mahlon's land and widow to the one individual more eligible to act than he. When this man declined, Boaz happily served as the kinsman-redeemer himself; he married Ruth, and their son Obed became the lawful heir of the land belonging to Naomi's husband and sons. His name continued the family line, and in fact he was a link in Christ's genealogy (see Matt. 1:5). Ruth's future and family were thus secured forever, and her name is recorded with honor in God's Word. Naomi's life's message had brought Ruth into God's family; Ruth in turn brought new life into Naomi's family. Now Naomi's friends could truly rejoice with her over her new son.

Even when she felt that God had dealt harshly with her, Naomi sought to know his will. Her discouragement never became disbelief. She kept her emotions in line with her sure knowledge of God. Because she did not hide her weakness, her strength strengthened others.

In our day, which stresses total openness in relationships, perhaps Christians have become too self-conscious and too fearful of being accused of hypocrisy. If we're not actually bubbling over with joy in the Lord at every moment, we hesitate to recommend him to others, and fail to appreciate his activity in the world around us. "Our walk must reflect our talk," we say, so we keep silent. "We cannot lead where we have never traveled," we mutter, and remain motionless. Satan is having a field day tying our tongues and hobbling our feet. "Praise the Lord, anyhow," is a popular but sadly feeble effort at Christian encouragement. Dear friends, we are missing myriad opportunities to glorify our God for his everlasting greatness and goodness! We need to learn from Naomi. While she was aware that her afflictions came from the Lord, her importance to him was affirmed by his lovingkindness.

Perhaps you have gone away full and come back empty in some aspect of your life. As you honestly evaluate your present position, whatever the pain, can you trust that God is not yet finished? Do not close your heart or your ears to his voice, to news of the

work he will yet do, to the fruit of his love and fulfillment of your life still ahead. And meanwhile, freely
tell others how God is working in your life right now.
They will very likely be drawn closer to him through
your truthful testimony.